MIRACLE AT
ZAKYNTHOS

MIRACLE AT
ZAKYNTHOS

THE ONLY GREEK JEWISH COMMUNITY
SAVED IN ITS ENTIRETY FROM ANNIHILATION

DENO SEDER

Philos Press / Washington, D.C.

Philos Press, LLC
P.O. Box 40277
Washington, D.C. 20016

Printed by CreateSpace, An Amazon.com Company
Cover design by Dick Bangham, Veronica Vannoy

Dedicated to the memory of the 70,000 Greek Jews
who died in the Holocaust
and to the "Righteous Among the Nations" of Greece

"Zakynthos is one of the few places in the world that, due to the heartfelt dedication of Bishop Chrysostomos and Mayor Loukas Carrer, succeeded in saving all the island's population from a terrible massacre. More than seventy years have passed since those horrible days when darkness covered the earth. I was happy to read about this ray of light. To my sorrow, there were too few of them during this time in history. The world today must learn from their hardship and behavior. I hope and pray that this book will become a beacon to humanity and inspire dedication to our fellow man."

Rabbi David Lau, Chief Rabbi of Israel
November 9, 2014

"In this well-researched and documented collection of firsthand accounts and historical texts, we witness the great spiritual stature of our not-so-distant forebears. Today, nearly seventy years after the liberation of Greece from German occupation, this book continues to serve as a painful, albeit powerful reminder of the intrepid bravery shown by the hierarchs, priests and Greek people in the face of inhumane threats against their Jewish neighbors in Greece. It is our prayer that this book will inspire and provide hope in our day, just as the actions of the islanders and the resulting salvation from death of the Greek Jewish population of Zakynthos bolstered the spirits of the Greek people in those dark and difficult times."

His All Holiness the Ecumenical Patriarch Bartholomew
January 2, 2015

TABLE OF CONTENTS

CHAPTER 1

WILL I SEE YOU TOMORROW?

*"They helped every one his neighbor;
and everyone said to his brother, be of good courage."*

Isaiah, 41:6

A sense of impending doom swept the Ionian island when the order came that every Jewish home was to display a yellow star on its door. The Italian occupation had been harsh, but this, the succeeding 1943 German occupation, was horrific.

The Greek Orthodox churches immediately began issuing false Christian identification papers and baptismal certificates to Jewish families. "I was no longer Malvina Messina. I became Varvara Stravridou. They were really good people. I felt they would never betray us."[1] Zakynthos Jews became accustomed to the fixed, exaggerated gaze of solemn, iconic Byzantine saints in the unlikely sanctuaries where the persecuted sought refuge. At great risk to themselves, the priests opened their churches and homes to their Jewish neighbors.

"The priests were a safe haven for Jews. We had better relations with the priests than the Christians did."[2] This life-saving Orthodox ethos emanated from the bishops, notably Archbishop Damaskinos of Athens and of all Greece and Bishop Chrysostomos of Zakynthos. The bishops implored their priests to instruct their parishioners that they had a moral obligation to help Jews. According to The International Raoul Wallenberg Foundation, Damaskinos was the only head of a European church to officially condemn the German occupation's treatment of Jews.[3] His letter of protest to the quisling prime minister of Greece read, in part:

> The Greek Orthodox Church and the Academic World of Greek People protest against the persecution...The Greek people were deeply grieved to learn that the German Occupation Authorities have already started to put into effect a program of gradual deportation of the Greek Jewish community...and that the first groups of deportees are already on their way to Poland.

In our national consciousness, all the children of Mother Greece are an inseparable unity: they are equal members of the national body irrespective of religion... Our common fate both in days of glory and in periods of national misfortune forged inseparable bonds between all Greek citizens, without exemption, irrespective of race...

Today we are deeply concerned with the fate of 60,000 of our fellow citizens who are Jews...we have lived together in both slavery and freedom, and we have come to appreciate their feelings, their brotherly attitude, their economic activity, and most important, their indefectible patriotism.[4]

The collaborationist Prime Minister, Konstantinos Logothetopoulos, did nothing to help. Damaskinos stated his intent to publish the letter, which prompted the local SS commander, Jürgen Stroop, to threaten execution by firing squad. The archbishop published the letter and promptly issued this famous response:

> According to the traditions of the Greek Orthodox Church, our prelates are hanged, not shot. Please respect our traditions![5]

The idea of a "national consciousness" professed by Archbishop Damaskinos humanized all Greeks, embraced Christians and Jews as an "inseparable unity," and condemned any attempt to discriminate or create racial or religious differences. The pathological perversion of this collective identity phenomenon is what led to the murder of six million Jews. Sociologist Bernhard Giesen describes it succinctly: "Perpetrators are human subjects who, by their own decision, dehumanized other subjects and, in doing so, did not only pervert the sovereign subjectivity of the victims but challenged also their own sacredness."[6]

In Greek society, racial and ethnic prejudice had little appeal, which explains why most Greeks found the German inhumane behavior alien and incomprehensible. The Greek novelist Giorgos Ioannou wrote:

> The Germans suddenly introduced into what today seems the almost idyllic

atmosphere of our unsuspecting, dusty Balkan culture all the abysmal medieval passions and idiocies of Gothic Europe.[7]

To the bishops and priests, these "medieval passions and idiocies" were depraved and immoral. With few exceptions, the holy men of Greece dedicated themselves to saving lives. Their courage was in stark contrast to the behavior of other European religious leaders, most notably the deafening silence and moral treachery of Pius XII. Historian John Cornwell wrote, "…it is clear that Pacelli [Pius XII] believed that the Jews had brought misfortune on their own heads; intervention on their behalf could draw the church into alliance with forces…whose ultimate aim was the destruction of the institutional church."[8]

The motivation for risking one's life to save another has become a popular topic of scholarly inquiry. As one Holocaust survivor and scholar wrote, "The most common reasons noted are religious beliefs, perceiving that it was one's duty to help another who was in trouble…obeying one's conscience or shame at not helping a neighbour."[9]

expressed similar sentiments more
quently four centuries earlier:

> No man is an island, intire of itself; every
> man is a peece of the Continent, A part of
> the maine...any man's death diminishes
> me, because I am involved in Mankinde;
> and therefore never send to know for
> whom the bell tolls; it tolls for thee.[10]

While the dicta and exhortations of Greek holy men protected people from capture and persecution, they could save neither Christian nor Jew from starvation. The famine that swept Greece during the occupation was a cruel denouement to yet another Greek tragedy. Historian Mark Mazower wrote, "Athens was to endure the worst scenes of starvation seen in occupied Europe outside the concentration camps."[11] The *New York Times* reported that an average of 500 Athenians were dying every day: "The principal streets of the Greek capital are littered with dead and dying...virtually all children are developing the wasted, bent, rickety legs and swollen bellies of incipient starvation."[12]

The International Red Cross supplied 15,000 tons of grain and 3,000 tons of dried vegetables per month for the period of the occupation, but that wasn't enough. The Greek government-in-exile and the private Greek War Relief organization funded the effort, but they soon ran out of money and the United States assumed the responsibility after January 1, 1943.

All of Greece suffered from the famine, forced as it was by unstated German policy to steal everything produced by Greek farmers, including wheat, butter, cheese, oil, olives, fruits and nuts, as well as most of the fish caught by Greek fishermen. The occupying forces consumed what they needed and sent the rest to Germany. During one year of the occupation alone, it was reported that over 500,000 tons of food and other commodities were shipped out of one city, Salonika (Thessaloniki) to Germany. [13] Estimated deaths from starvation varied -- during the first year of the occupation in Greece, the Red Cross estimated that 250,000 people had died of starvation, while the BBC reported as many as 500,000 deaths.

Exorbitant prices for coal and wood meant that homes were not properly heated during the winter, resulting in colds, flu and TB, compounded by malnutrition, which resulted in even more deaths.

The famine spread to Zakynthos, where eleven-year-old Erkanas Tsezana and his family had to struggle to survive. "What disappointed me most at the time," recalled Erkanas fifty-six years later, "was that at bar mitzvahs, we had nothing to treat people with, nothing but a cup of raisins."[14]

Erkanas and his family lost everything soon after the Nazis occupied the island. Once middle-class fabric merchants with a shop, the family was forced to learn how to live off the land to survive. They bought some sheep and goats, grew corn, squash and potatoes, sold their jewelry to buy flour, and managed to survive while many starved. "Our priority was to figure out how we were going to survive the next day, what we were going to eat, how we could find two kilos of flour so we could feed the whole family for the next few days."[15]

A neighbor, Raphael Constantinos, was a few years older than Erkanas and the oldest of six boys in a Jewish family. When there was no food, he was assigned a grim task. "I had to pick and boil grass with olive oil and lemon. Sometimes people got bloated and died from eating the grasses. The city would send a cart to pick up the bodies."[16]

Erkanas and Raphael learned to live with hunger. Living with fear was another story. For them and for all the 275 Greek Jews on Zakynthos, the fear of exposure was constant, palpable and terrifying. "Life had changed. It was like lighting struck our ghetto. It was traumatic."[17]

"Some German soldiers kicked in our door and started beating me," recalled Hertsel Matsa, who was nineteen at the time. "I was able to escape and hide in some hay bales. I could hear them shouting, 'Where is that Jew? We will kill him.' I learned later that they beat our Christian neighbors because they thought they helped me escape."[18] He stayed hidden in the hay bales until the next day. A curfew prevented Jews from leaving their homes from 5 p.m. to 7 a.m. the next morning.

Before the Germans occupied Zakynthos, there was some hope in spite of pervasive fear. The Italian soldiers had grown weary of the war. They were exhausted and eagerly anticipated the end of the war and return home.

Anastasios and Rubini Tetradis lived on a small, isolated farm in Gaitani, about ten miles from Zakynthos city. They had recently lost one child, an infant who died of pneumonia, and struggled to raise and feed the other five children. The family had a few cows, goats, and chickens, some olive trees, and a strong will to survive the famine and the occupation. The children had no toys and amused themselves by playing with the chickens.

Because of their isolation, they had never seen an Italian or German soldier, until the day Rubini saw someone hiding behind some bushes near the animal barn. She ran to find Anastasios, who grabbed his shotgun and confronted the intruder, shouting and cursing at him in Greek. Anastasios was a good and decent man, a simple man with little education. He was a devout Greek Orthodox Christian, but if his family was threatened, he would not hesitate to pull the trigger. The peasant farmer demanded that the intruder show himself, and what came out surprised him. A very young man, an Italian solider, crawled out from behind the bushes, sobbing. He babbled in Italian while Anastasios shouted in Greek. There was no communication between these two, but judging from the Italian's wet and ragged uniform and gaunt appearance, Anastasios felt no threat. The sobbing continued. Feeling pity for this wretched creature, Anastasios put his gun down, opened his arms and embraced the young man.

The family took in the soldier, fed him, clothed him and had him sleep under their own bed in case the Germans would come looking for Italian soldiers or Jewish citizens.

Several days later, things got really complicated. Anastasios found six more Italian soldiers hiding along the muddy bank of a nearby stream. They were in even worse shape than the first young soldier. They were filthy and their uniforms were in shreds. Two of the men were nearly naked and most could barely walk. "Ella," Anastasios ordered, and the men rose slowly and followed him to the farm, where they were shown their new temporary quarters, the animal barn.

Rubini and one of her daughters cut up some bed sheets and made rudimentary clothing for the men. A large hole was dug in the barn with a trap door. This was where the men hid and slept for nearly two months until the German occupation on the island became too dangerous for everyone.

In 1962, when the youngest child, Takis, was twelve-years-old, his father told him the story. "This is who we are. This is how we treat people. This is how we live our lives." Takis, choking back tears, recalled that his father grabbed him by the ears and shouted, "Remember what I told you."[19]

When Mussolini was unexpectedly overthrown by a palace coup in July, 1943, British liaison officers got Greek resistance fighters together with demoralized Italian commanders. And when the news came that Italy had surrendered, Italian soldiers and Greek civilians came together to celebrate. Mountain villagers came down to join the riotous celebrations. Within hours, all fascist flags and emblems disappeared. In Athens, the scene was Felliniesque – a surreal, endless street market festival featuring an incongruous commerce – Italians selling food and weapons to Greeks. Items included guns, hand grenades, motorbikes, blankets, boots, furniture, typewriters, even cars. But with reflexive speed, the Germans quickly turned off the lights, for the party was over. They gave the Italians an ultimatum: continue to fight under German command or get on a train to a POW camp in Yugoslavia. The Italians choose neither.

The Zakynthians had many friends and relatives living on Cephalonia, a nearby island directly north. Small groups of armed Greeks had joined the Italians to fight the Germans on that island, but the outcome was deadly for the insurgents – 4,905 men were captured and executed by firing squad. Their bodies were dumped into the sea. One material benefit resulted from this terrible event and the Italian collapse: "…it contributed men, arms and psychological encouragement to the armed resistance to German rule. Across the country, large stocks of weapons and supplies fell in the hands of the *andartes* [guerrillas]."[20]

The German displacement of the Italians further exacerbated the nation's economic catastrophe. The Germans exploited the economic resources in other occupied countries of Western Europe (France, Belgium, the Netherlands, Denmark and Norway) but did not destroy the existing economic productive capacity of those nations nor did they change the monetary mechanism. This was not the case in Greece, where the Germans plundered the economy with indifference and impunity.

The occupiers had two major economic interests in Greece – foodstuffs and mineral ores, especially chrome, bauxite, manganese, molybdenum, and nickel, which were vital in making alloys for munitions. In 1942, 62,000 tons of chrome ore came from mines in two cities alone. Most of it was shipped to Germany. The year before, the Germans confiscated 305 tons of silk cocoons and 5,200 tons of wool, crippling one of Greece's most important industries and leaving thousands unemployed. [21] The country's entire tobacco crop was seized, the Greek merchant marine was decimated, cars and trucks were seized, businesses were purchased at a fraction of their worth, and food stocks were taken to either feed the occupation troops or for shipment to Axis troops in North Africa. Between May 1 and September 30, 1941, 45,700,000 *Reichsmarks* worth of goods had been exported to Germany, and by the end of the year, the total had reached 150,000,000. [22]

The economic collapse of the country hit Greek Jews especially hard. In Salonika, for example, Jews were prominent business leaders and professionals.

Jewish concerns had established the first water, gas and electric companies and in the earlier part of the twentieth century, they imported twenty-six percent of Salonika's industrial goods.[23]

There were two broad categories of Greek Jews: Romaniotes and Sephardim. The Romaniotes were more indigenous, having arrived during the first century AD from Palestine following the destruction of the second Jerusalem temple by the Romans in AD 70. Many Jewish communities in Greece had ancient origins that have been lost and forgotten over time. Near Mykonos, for example, is the small island of Delos, reputed to have been the birthplace of Apollo and Artemis. Delos was a sacred island in ancient Greece, a cultural center as well as a holy sanctuary that had been inhabited since the third millennium BC. In 1912, archaeologists discovered a synagogue on the island, with its origin dating between 150 and 128 BC.

The Sephardim came much later than the Romaniotes -- in the late fifteenth and early sixteenth centuries, having been expelled by the Catholic Church in Spain, Portugal, France and Italy. The Sephardim spoke Ladino (*Judeo-*

Espanyol), derived from Old Spanish and influenced by Hebrew and Aramaic. The Romaniotes spoke Greek and had assimilated into Greek culture and society. Most of the Jewish community of Zakynthos was Romaniote. They spoke the same language, had similar values, lived and worked together peacefully with their Christian neighbors.

Christians and Jews on the island shared a history and culture that evolved from its golden era during the Mycenaean period (1600 BC – 1100 BC). In the seventeenth century, Zakynthos developed its own special form of theater, know as the *Omilia,* performed in public places by actors and singers. A great musical tradition on the island flourished over the years and exerted its influence over all of Greece. The country's first music school was established on Zakynthos in 1815, introducing opera and operetta to the rest of Greece. Even during the years of occupation, vestigial harmonies reverberated on the island.

A young prodigy as a violinist, Tsezana and his Jewish band were favorites at Christian events, including church functions, public festivals, even prayer services honoring saints. "We played mostly

Bach. Once we were treated to coffee and paximathia [Greek cookies] after playing and I got to meet the mayor and the bishop. The bishop said I could have a second paximathi and the guy next to me asked why I got to have a second paximathi, and I remember the bishop saying, 'Because he's a Jew,' and I thought how awesome that was, and that's the kind of relationship we had with the Greek Christian Zakynthians."[24]

The nobility of the Greek Orthodox clergy during the occupation has been well documented, as have the attitudes of most Greek Christians during this difficult period. "...the vast majority of Greeks had come to regard their country's Jews as compatriots and a vital element of the nation's human assets."[25] And historically, the Romaniote Jews of Zakynthos (as well as those from Patras, Corfu, Volos and Athens) fought with their Greek Christian comrades in many wars and conflicts, including the Greco-Turkish War of 1897.

There is much evidence that Greek Jews went into the mountains to join guerrilla bands such as ELAS (Greek People's Liberation Army), the dominant resistance group in Greece. This was risky business – raiding German silos for distribution to farmers, destroying roads and bridges, committing acts of sabotage and some unspeakable brutalities. Greek Jewish women also went into the mountains to serve as nurses, while others organized companies of uniformed women *andartes*. Sarika Y was a captain in a resistance company:

> This is my country. I was born and raised here. The Greeks are my people, their fight is my fight. This is where I belong.[26]

An Athenian newspaper reported:

> Athens, Oct, 23, 1944 (ONA by Wireless) – Sarika Y-- 18-year-old Jewish Greek girl…is the captain of a company of uniformed women Andartes…wearing a pair of British soldier boots and cap, jacket and culottes uniform made from an American blanket, she leads her company daily in doing whatever the Andarte regiment to which she is attached orders.[27]

Another young Greek Jewish woman from Corfu, known only as Minorvo, joined a guerilla group called EPON (the National Patriotic Youth

Organization) and took part in numerous actions against the Germans, including the detonation of a German-occupied building in Salonika. She was caught, conceded her guilt and shouted to the judges at her trial when sentenced to death: "I was born a Jew, I am a Jew, and I will die a Jew." She was shot to death on the following day.[28]

ELAS was the armed resistance movement of EAM (National Liberation Front), which had been the only Greek political organization to actively and systematically arrange for the protection of Jews during the occupation. Virtually every Jew who survived the occupation had some form of contact with EAM.[29]

As the first true mass social movement in Greek history, EAM established its own government, courts and schools. About 650 Jews served in the EAM/ELAS resistance and were respected and valued due to their training, literacy and patriotism.

The ELAS military wing was by far the largest guerilla organization in Greece. It operated completely independent of Allied support and carried out the most attacks on German units. The collaborationist government propaganda denounced the resistance fighters as the "Bolsheviks of the Greek mountains," as well as "criminals, gangsters [and] anarchists." [30] Government newspapers tried to spread the hysteria and paranoia by claiming that an Allied victory "would produce a victory for communism by spreading 'pan-Slavism' to the Aegean [and] that EAM/ELAS was a tool of international communism and that it had used patriotism and nationalism to gain the support of the Greek people."[31]

A different portrait of the guerillas was painted by British historian Richard Cobb:

> For if the proud, hungry guerillas of ELAS were radical in their social aspirations, they were clearly democrats so far as politics was concerned. Their decision to take up arms was an assertion of everything that was most admirable in the Greek spirit – a fierce patriotism, a refusal to calculate where matters of honour were concerned, a stoic acceptance of enormous hardship and a determination to act together against overwhelming odds.[32]

The Greek *andartes* were heroic warriors. They are credited with one the most spectacular partisan victories of World War II, the battle of Karalokou, on the southern slope of Mt. Olympus. Five Jewish families were hiding in some barns in the canyon when they were surprised early one morning by an SS battalion. Four men escaped and ran toward the mountain to inform the partisans. Three were gunned down and killed by the Germans. The fourth man was able to escape and found his way to the guerilla mountain camp, where an ELAS battalion of about 150 men went into action. A Greek Jewish partisan vividly recalled what happened that day:

> I can see a great number of people with helmets and military uniforms moving right and left. They are Germans, a whole battalion of them...without wasting any time our forces were deployed on the cliffs surrounding the area of the barns. We occupied the high ground so fast that as soon as the order to open fire was given and the singing of our machineguns commenced, dozens of Germans fell dead

and wounded. Slowly and without reducing our heavy fire, we started descending, surrounding the Germans in a smaller circle. The Germans started to fire back, but we did not stop. Our accurate fire brings down more Germans. Soon the enemy is seized by panic...Some surrender, others try to hide, others abandon their guns and try to escape.[33]

Another partisan witness offered this account:

The Germans were encircled and ambushed from the sides of a canyon. German planes came to help, but the terrain of this gorge was such that they were ineffective. Some Germans managed to escape, but those who remained found a tragic end. About 150 Germans were killed, 78 were wounded and 14, including the German commander, became prisoners. Ten of the prisoners were executed because they attempted to disarm their guards. The remaining were also put to death. That is a total of 242 German dead. Partisan losses were eleven dead and ten wounded.[34]

Hitler sent instructions to Field Marshal Wilhelm Keitel to use the most brutal means necessary to fight the *andartes.* Keitel issued this order on December 16, 1942:

> The troops are therefore authorized and ordered in this struggle to take any measures without restriction even against women and children if these are necessary for success. [Humanitarian] considerations of any kind are a crime against the German nation.[35]

Most Greek Jews were completely unaware that by 1943 and 1944, millions of European Jews had been killed, but the Greek resistance fighters knew the terrible truth and in January of 1943, EAM made and circulated the following proclamation:

> For all the Greek people, brothers and sisters: A new crime is planned by the conqueror. We face a new demonstration of fascist brutality which this time affects the Jewish members of the Greek people. The bloody conqueror prepares one of the most formidable and disgusting pogroms against the Greek Jews,

like those which were organized in Germany and Poland. In Salonika, thousands of innocent women and children are threatened with executions, mass slaughter and concentration camps of the horrible Gestapo...This new crime is not directly only against the Jews, but against the Greek people, because the Greek Jews are a part of our people, because their fate is connected with the fate of the entire Greek people.[36]

Dimitrios Katevatis, a medical doctor, was a resistance leader who, according to his son, Nicholas, had a tense encounter with a German officer during the early days of the occupation. At risk of being arrested, he told the officer, "As the leader of the underground with more than 800 armed men in the hills, I must warn you about the dire consequences of deporting the Jews."[37]

Katevatis confessed to his son that he was bluffing the Germans, since the resistance at that stage of the war had only handguns, rifles and limited ammunition. "There is no case of attacking a well-seasoned German battalion. I just boasted...As for the Jews, whenever abused I will always protect them...Do you know that unlike

Greeks, no Jew committed murder, no stabbing, no beating. There is no Jew criminal in the jail of the island. They are extremely good people, and I am happy that I protected them."[38] Years after the war, Nicholas Katevatis wrote of his father, "It proves that people without the slightest interest, without a moment of hesitation traded the safety and life of themselves and their family to protect the Jews. It sounds like fiction, but it is true history."[39]

◆   ◆   ◆

An often-overlooked minority persecuted and killed by the Germans were the Romani or Roma (commonly and pejoratively called Gypsies). Like the Sephardic Jews, they also came to Greece during the 15th and 16th centuries. A nomadic people, the Romani on Zakynthos and throughout most of Greece were Greek Orthodox and spoke Greek in addition to their Romani language. They had Greek names and a Greek identity, but to Germans, they were thought to be "incurably mentally ill." In 1920, two Germans, a psychiatrist and a judge, wrote a book promoting euthanasia called *The Eradication of Lives Undeserving of Life* in which they asserted that Romanies had a transmitted genetic disease that made them "underserving of life," a phrase that was incorporated into law just four months after Hitler became Chancellor of the Third Reich.[40]

The Germans in Greece felt no compunction about killing a Romani for any reason, since back home in Germany, it was not illegal to kill a Romani. "[T]here were sometimes 'Gypsy hunts' in which Romanies were tracked down and killed like wild animals; forests were set on fire to drive out any Romanies who might have been hiding there."[41]

The small group of Romanies on Zakynthos had no idea that the first mass genocidal action of the Holocaust took place in January, 1940 when 250 Romani children from Brno, Czechoslovakia were murdered in Buchenwald. These innocents were used as guinea-pigs to test the efficacy of the Zyklon-B cyanide gas crystals that were later used in the gas chambers.[42] Somewhere between 500,000 and a million Romani were killed by the Germans.

At the Nuremberg trials, the mass murder of the Roma was not addressed, nor were any Romani witnesses called. The first commemoration of the

Romani holocaust was on April 14, 1994 at the United States Holocaust Museum and to this day, just one Nazi, Ernst-August König, a former Auschwitz guard, has been prosecuted and sentenced specifically for crimes against Romani. On September 18, 1991, at age seventy-one, he hung himself in his German prison cell.

Isabel Fonseca wrote in her book, *Bury Me Standing, The Gypsies and Their Journey:*

> The Second World War and its traumas are certainly within memory; but there is no tradition of commemoration, or even of discussion...Under the Nazis, the Gypsies were the only group apart from the Jews who were slated for extermination on grounds of race. It is a story that remains almost unknown – even to many Gypsies who survived it.[43]

The Romani were helpful to the Greek resistance primarily in the area of communications. Because they were nomadic and moved from town to town, they were able to get information and pass it along to the guerillas.

27

Few Romani actually joined the guerillas, but a number of Greek Jews did. Young Erkanas Tsezana admired the bravery and kindness of the *andartes*. "One Saturday, the guerrillas came down from the mountains and had a confrontation with the Germans. There was machine gun fire right outside our house. We were terrified. It was always like that. We lived with fear, went to bed with fear, woke up with fear. We didn't know if we would live or die. Every night when the sun went down, I would ask: 'Will I see you tomorrow?'" [44]

CHAPTER 2

Ethos

"There is neither Jew nor Gentile…"

Galatians 3:28

The young altar boy was tormented. He so earnestly wanted to talk with God, but his pious, pleading entreaties went unanswered, and as he suspected, unheard. At the tender age of twelve, Dimitrios had nearly memorized the entire divine liturgy. Most troubling was the priest's incantation following the congregation's recitation of the Nicene Creed. As the choir sang, "We lift up our hearts to the Lord. It is meet and right…" the priest, in the altar with his back to the congregation, would intone, *sotto voce*:

Thou art God ineffable, incomprehensible, invisible, inconceivable…

"What kind of God is this?" thought Dimitrios. Granted he's invisible, but a God incapable of being expressed in words? A God we can't understand or even imagine? And why is the priest whispering? Was the truth so terrifying that it could not be spoken out loud or chanted by the choir or the *psaltis?*

At least Jesus was a comprehensible, conceivable being. But why must the priest promise Jesus not to tell his secrets?

I will not speak of the mystery to thine enemies...

And who were these "enemies"? And why were they enemies? These questions were problematic, but forty years later, Dimitrios, who grew up to become Bishop Chrysostomos of Zakynthos, had a new set of problems, the most immediate of which was the German Luger aimed at his head.

Chrysostomos loved the social character of the Orthodox Church. It was an attitude that allowed him to work for the transformation of society. This attitude has prevailed with increasing popularity since World War II, despite criticism and contention that Orthodoxy has no social character, that it preaches only salvation of the faithful and is indifferent to daily life and social problems.

Critics postulate that this ancient church, replete with rituals, clouds of incense and primitive icons, is irrelevant, anachronistic and does little to improve the condition of mankind. Yet in many parts of Greece during the occupation, the social character of the church manifestly exerted itself into the daily lives of Christians and Jews alike.

The Orthodox Church's social character has been described as having evolved from a belief that "[e]very relationship with God which ignores one's neighbors leads to a kind of individual piety centered on a God who is not the God of the Judaeo-Christian tradition, but a creation of the wishes and fantasies of man."[45] The Greek bishops and priests did not ignore their neighbors. They did not subscribe to a "faith only" dogma and were not restrained by canon law.

The Great Schism of 1054 was an historic event that led to the ultimate separation of the Eastern Christian Church led by the Patriarch of Constantinople, Michael Cerularius, and the head of the Western Church led by Pope Leo IX. To punctuate and finalize their estrangement, the two men mutually excommunicated each other. The ban was lifted in 1965 when Greek Orthodox Patriarch Athenagoras and Catholic Pope Paul VI decided that after nine hundred years, it was time for some interfaith brotherly love.

The Schism freed the Greek bishops and priests from the imperative of following an archaic Roman legalistic spirit as the path to salvation. To many Orthodox holy men and thinkers, this was an essential difference between their faith and Roman Catholicism. It was a difference that cultivated tolerance, understanding and respect between Jews and Christians. It was a difference that opened church doors to Jewish musicians who performed during wedding ceremonies and even during Orthodox religious holidays such as the festival honoring the island's patron saint. It was a difference that granted the bishops and priests a sanction and a compulsion to speak out and save lives during the Holocaust in Greece.

Similarly, the Orthodox ethical principle of *ekonomia*, the precursor to situational ethics, gave the bishops what amounted to a theological "get out of jail free" card. Originally denoting maintenance of the household, *ekonomia* allowed bishops to determine the moral and ethical consequences of following the law, and if those consequences were deemed to be harmful, the laws were ignored. Perhaps some of the church's early thinkers interpreted St. Paul's exhortation as a situational *carte blanche:* "Work out your own salvation with fear and trembling, for it is God who works in you to will and to act in order to fulfill his good purpose." (Phil. 2:12-13.)

What a prominent Orthodox theologian and ethicist calls "the mind of the church"[46] avoids facile historical reductionism and further explains why the bishops and priests acted the way they did:

> The Orthodox Church has a very strong tradition of relationships. The bishops and clergy of Zakynthos had personal relationships with everyone on the island. To them, under the circumstance of the German occupation, relationship was more important than law, and their beliefs, practices, worship, ethos and ethical stances led them to issue fake baptismal and marriage certificates to their Jewish friends and neighbors. They

fulfilled what they believed was the human purpose. It was a fundamental expression of love.[47]

This theology of relationships is recurrent as a shepherd metaphor in Orthodoxy. (There are ten million sheep in Greece – nearly one per person. Plus five million goats.) The prayer at a bishop's consecration reads:

Grant, o Christ, that this man, who has been appointed a steward of the episcopal grace, may become an imitator of thee, the true shepherd, by laying down his life for the sheep...

Historically, the Orthodox Church has been concerned with the here and now, as well as the hereafter, and with the affairs of the state and the welfare of its citizens. This is a totality that has been embraced by a church concerned about social improvement and the betterment of our physical, as well as spiritual lives. As one Orthodox scholar put it, "The Church is not a museum of saints for the service of saints...but is available to everyone...no one is abandoned to his or her fate."[48]

During the Holocaust, Bishops Chrysostomos, Damaskinos and others made no distinction between Christian and Jew in defending their flock. In their minds, *"There is neither Jew nor Gentile."* (Gal. 3:28) An interpretation of Romans 7:5 by an Orthodox bishop reflects this ethical disposition:

> We should each of us look upon our neighbour's experiences as if they were our own. We should suffer with our neighbour in everything and weep with him, and should behave as if we were inside his body; and if any trouble befalls him, we should feel as much distress on his account as we would for ourselves.[49]

Unlike the sentiments found in Romans 7:5, there was little benevolence toward Jews to be found among European Christian hierarchy. Catholic and Protestant culpability for the Holocaust has been offered as a thesis for unintended consequences, resulting in the death of millions. "That anti-Judaism became a powerful force for evil in the world is an example of what social scientists term the law of unintended consequences [which] fueled a long tradition of intolerance, hatred, and violence..."[50]

The yellow star, restrictions on movement and freedom and other anti-Jewish measures had direct antecedents in church laws and practices. The Fourth Lateran Council decreed in 1213 that Jews must wear distinctive markings on their clothing. The Synod of Breslau decreed in 1267 that Jews must live in ghettos. One Holocaust scholar, Raul Hilberg, identified thirteen other canon laws with direct parallels to Nazi race laws. The church gave the Third Reich a justification for persecution and murder.

Two of the churches earliest anti-Semites were St. Augustine and St. John Chrysostom, both fourth century church leaders. Augustine originated the Christian just war theory (*bellum iustum*) which endured through the centuries so as to influence most German bishops and priests who supported Hitler and his war effort. Augustine blamed Jews for the death of Christ. In his "On the Creed: A Sermon to Catechumens," he offers this rebuke,

which was to influence Christian thought and
prejudice for centuries:

> The Jews hold him, the Jews insult him,
> the Jews bind him, crown him with thorns,
> dishonor him with spitting, scourge him,
> overwhelm him with revilings, hang him
> upon the tree, pierce him with a
> spear...The Jews killed him.[51]

Chrysostom, who served as Archbishop of
Constantinople, offered a more rabid, hysterical
invective against Jews:

> The Synagogue is a brothel, a hiding place
> for unclean beasts...Jews are the most
> worthless of all men [who] are lecherous,
> greedy and rapacious...perfidious
> murderers of Christ and for killing God
> there is no expiation possible, no
> indulgence or pardon. Christians may
> never cease vengeance...Jews must live in
> servitude forever...God always hated
> Jews. It is incumbent upon all Christians
> to hate Jews.[52]

Augustine and Chrysostom. What saints these.

The architect of Protestant reformation, Martin Luther, was a virulent anti-Semite whose writings could have been a blueprint for Hitler's final solution. In his hateful, disgusting diatribe, "On the Jews and Their Lies," written in 1543, Luther accused Jews of murder, kidnapping children, poisoning wells and other preposterous and undocumented crimes (including using the blood of Christian children to make matzo). The Jews were "venomous serpents and devil's children...the most vehement enemies of Christ." This is the advice Martin Luther gave to his Christian followers:

> What shall we Christians do with this rejected and condemned people, the Jews? Since they live among us, we dare not tolerate their conduct...First, to set fire to their synagogues or schools and to bury and cover with dirt whatever will not burn, so that no man will ever again see a stone or cinder of them...Second, I advise that their houses also be razed and destroyed. For they pursue in them the same aims as in their synagogues.[53]

Twenty-five years later, in 1568, the Greek Orthodox Patriarch, Metrophanes III of Constantinople, presented a different theological point of view from Luther's vulgar invective. The Patriarch was an outspoken advocate for tolerance and justice for members of other faiths. In one strongly worded encyclical, he condemned the mistreatment of Jews in Crete:

> Injustice...regardless to whomever acted upon or performed against, is still injustice. The unjust person is never relieved of the responsibility of these acts under the pretext that the injustice is done against a heterodox and not to a believer. As our Lord Jesus Christ in the Gospels said do not oppress or accuse anyone falsely; do not make any distinction or give room to the believers to injure those of another belief.[54]

Five centuries before Luther and Metrophanes III, Pope Benedict VIII ordered the execution of Jews that he believed were responsible for causing hurricanes and earthquakes. Jews were also blamed for causing the Black Death (1348-49) and for desecrating the sacraments of holy communion, purportedly to recrucify Christ. This provoked German and Austrian citizens to massacre an estimated 100,000 Jews and obliterate 140 Jewish communities.[55]

Nearly 50,000 Spanish Jews were killed during the Spanish Inquisition and approximately 300,000 were expelled from the country in 1492.

In the eighteenth century, Pope Benedict XIV wrote with alarm about the growing number of Jews in Poland, assuring his followers that the Catholic Church would "...cooperate energetically and effectively with those whose combined authority and power are appropriate to remove this stain of shame from Poland."[56]

And in the twentieth century, Pope Benedict XVI, through a subtle act of linguistic sublimation, restored an old Latin prayer back into the Catholic service calling for the forgiveness and conversion of Jews, rekindling the "Jews killed Jesus" theme. This was denounced by all of Italy's rabbis and prominent Jewish leaders worldwide. Popes throughout history have chanted this malicious melody. In the thirteenth century, Pope Innocent III wrote:

The Jews' guilt of the crucifixion of Jesus consigned them to perpetual servitude, and like Cain, they are to be wanderers and fugitives...the Jews will not dare to raise their necks, bowed under the yoke of perpetual slavery, against the reverence of the Christian faith.[57]

Christian complicity and culpability for the Holocaust is a sad truth of history. Many church leaders remained as mute after the war as Pius XII had been during the war. There were exceptions, however. In 1994, a group of Hungarian bishops issued a statement acknowledging their church's complicity for the Holocaust:

[Catholics] who through fear, cowardice, or opportunism, failed to raise their voices against the mass humiliation, deportation and murder of their Jewish neighbors must also be held responsible, and before God we now ask forgiveness for this failure.[58]

The worst genocide in human history had deep roots. Deborah Lipstadt, a professor of Jewish history, contends that it took "German National

Socialism to pull from the thick soil of Jew hatred the means to murder millions. However, without a pre-existing animus that was so deeply ingrained in Western culture--both secular and religious, enlightened and unenlightened--the Nazis could never have accomplished what they did."[59]

The Greek Orthodox Christians of Zakynthos did not inherit the centuries-old institutionalized Catholic and Protestant anti-Semitism. A few Jewish citizens felt the lingering vestiges of ancient antipathy, but for the most part, the Jews and Christians of the island felt connected to one another. They were friends and neighbors. There was an unspoken bond of trust, especially during the darkest days of the occupation. Survivor testimonies underscored this trust:

> All the Greek villagers knew where we were hiding, but nobody said a word, nobody. [60] (Shlomo Amar)

> They were really good people. They saved us. They never betrayed us.[61] (Malvina Messina)

The bishop loved us. And we loved him.[62]
(Hertsel Matsa)

Perhaps the real miracle of Zakynthos was that not one of the 42,000 Christians on the island said a word to the Nazis about where the Jews were being hidden. While historians may argue about the reasons why, the Orthodox ethos is probably the best explanation. Orthodox Christians were given moral and ethical direction and latitude for freedom of choice and behavior. It was given by their bishops and priests, having been decided and memorialized by ecumenical councils, hierarchical encyclicals, ethical teachings and pastoral guidelines. Often referred to as the "ought" aspect of the Church, it is a core part of the Church's ethical teaching and is preached to the faithful as a worldview and as a personal commitment. Simply, it refers to what a person ought and ought not to do. "The 'ought' aspect...is rooted in the affirmations of the faith. All Orthodox Christians are considered free in making moral choices. The tradition guides and directs, but does not coerce..."[63]

Not all Greek Orthodox Christians, before, during and after the war, made good moral choices however. Greek Jews had been a protected minority citizenry since the passage of a law to that effect in 1920. This legal status gave them a sense of a distinctly *Greek* Jewish identity. It was a catalyst for the cultural assimilation of thousands of Jews, resulting in the realization of a true Greek Jewish culture.[64] In Salonika, for example, the Jewish community which called itself the Israelite Community of Salonika, began referring to itself as the Greek Jewish Community of Salonika.

In 1927, an anti-Semitic organization, *Ethniki Enosis Elias* (Hellas Patriotic Union) was founded in Salonika. It was known to its followers as the Triple Epsilon (EEE). To others, it was known as *Ellines Exontosate Evraious* (Greeks Eliminate Jews).[65] It recruited more than 3,000 members.

On June 24, 1931, a mob of about one hundred ultranationalist youth attacked the Jewish Maccabees sports organization headquarters, wounding a number of people. Five days later, a rabid anti-Semitic newspaper called *Makedonía,* ran a large headline urging its readers to "Finish [the Jews] Off!"[66] That night, a crazed mob of more than a thousand set fire to the Campbell district, an area of Salonika housing poor Jewish families. Violence quickly spread to other Jewish neighborhoods where homes and synagogues were looted and burned.

There were many anti-Jewish collaborators and perpetrators throughout Greece during the war, but this, the actions of Greek "Christian" nationalist extremists in 1931 was the worst incident of anti-Semitism in the history of Greece. The Prime Minister, Eleuthérios Venizélos, acted quickly. Martial law was declared and an army battalion was sent to protect the Jewish neighborhoods of Salonika. Ten years later, the Germans reestablished the EEE in Salonika as part of their overall strategy to bring political and economic ruin to Greece.

EEE was one of three collaborationist groups. The others were the Greek Nazis, an insignificant group, and the Greek Fascist Party, which had been around since 1931 and had about 50,000 supporters, including some prominent people such as a former minister to Germany, the Governor General of Thrace, a Vice Admiral and some politicians and professional people. The party's leadership sent a telegram to Hitler apologizing for Greece having been seduced by "Anglo-Jewish propaganda."[67]

In the summer of 1941, most of the collaborators (with the exception of the EEE) merged their groups to form the *Ethniko-Sosialistike Patriotike Organosis* (ESPO—National Socialist Political Organization). Dr. Spyros Sterodemas became head of the new party. As a member of the medical board of former dictator Ioannis Metaxas, Sterodemas got into trouble with some prostitutes and was forced to resign. The scandal led him to a new career as a fascist leader and amateur philosopher. His peripatetic postulations included the linking of Nazism to the laws of Lycurgus and Plato. "Since Lycurgus and Plato were Greek, their descendants in the twentieth century could become great by reapplying these old principles."[68] His philosophy gained few adherents and virtually no popular support. On September 22, 1942, Sterodemas was in the ESPO headquarters giving a lecture to a group of fellow collaborators. A young anti-Nazi, Kostas Perrikos, entered the building and blew it up, killing a number of people, including Sterodemas.

Four months later, in January of 1943, the Germans felt they had established good working relationships with Greek government collaborators. And they had. They went so far as to provide the Greek collaborationist government in Athens with close to two months' notification of the deportations to Auschwitz.

> Günter Altenburg, the *de facto* German ambassador, met with the collaborationist prime minister, Constantine Logothetopoulos, to inform him of the impending expulsion of the Greek Jews to Poland. After their discussion, Altenburg told Berlin to expect "no difficulties" from Logothetopoulos.[69]

The Germans experienced difficulties, however, from many of the Greek Orthodox priests and bishops, whose faith and humanity guided them to resist the occupiers. But just as there are political differences during an enemy occupation, there are differences in belief among people of faith regarding atrocities against innocent people, and differences among faiths as to war itself. In addition to their divergent views on issues such as canon law, social character and relationships, Orthodoxy and Catholicism differ in thought as regards the theory of the "just war." The Orthodox Church views much of the violence and war in the Bible as eschatological allegories. The Church never bought into the "just war" politics and it has seldom, if ever, been reflected in the writings of its best thinkers. It's just not part of the Orthodox consciousness. That's not to say that the Church is naïve, unworldly or pacifist. After all, the divine liturgy in Orthodox churches around the world asks for the Almighty's blessing of the armed forces. But justifying military action as God-given, or God-blessed or in God's name seems, shall we say, "unChristianlike." To most enlightened biblical scholars, the "just war" amounts to a fundamentalist, wrongheaded misinterpretation of scripture. As one scholar admonished, "Those who believe they can find glorification of righteous war in the teachings of Jesus have made some serious mistakes in their interpretation of the New Testament."[70]

When the Nazis began to supplant the Italians on Zakynthos, trepidation swept the island. The Nazi malevolence was appalling. Whereas the

Italians stole food and occasionally beat up someone, the Nazis shot people, hung people from olive trees and burned entire villages. They tried to get Greek Christians to adopt anti-Semitic attitudes by promising to distribute Jewish property and other possessions among the Christians. According to the Greek Ministry of Foreign Affairs, "[n]o Greek voluntarily presented himself to request a house or any other asset belonging to a Jew."[71] Christians and Jews knew they were in this together, and would live or die together. Sadly, tragically, that sense of belonging did not prevail in many other nations.

◆ ◆ ◆

The Greek word *logos* has been used among philosophers and theologians to mean word, thought, principle or speech. Heraclitus may have been the first to use the word to refer to a rational divine intelligence. In Christianity, the *logos* doctrine has much significance:

In the beginning was the Word, and the Word was with God, and the Word was God. (John, 1:1)

During World War II, the Serbian Orthodox Church didn't get the "word" about God. Or they had trouble with the translation from the Greek. In the twisted, unabashed Serbian anti-Orthodox lexicon, the meaning of "word" was not God, it was "collaboration." The mentality this church displayed during the Nazi occupation, using Heraclitus' reference, was neither "rational" nor "divine." It was a perversion of all that was good and holy and life affirming about the Orthodox faith. It was evil incarnate.

The Serbian Orthodox Church openly and shamefully collaborated with the Nazis. While Bishop Damaskinos of Athens wrote letters protesting against the persecution of the nation's Jewish citizens ("In our national consciousness, all the children of Mother Greece are an inseparable unity."), the first three signers of "An Appeal to the Serbian Nation" calling for loyalty to the occupying Nazis were bishops of the Serbian Orthodox Church.

While Greek Bishops Damaskinos, Chrysostomos and others were issuing false baptismal certificates to their Jewish citizens, the Serbian Orthodox holy men did not. On January 30, 1942, Metropolitan Josif, the acting head of the Holy Synod of the Serbian Orthodox Church, sentenced thousands of Serbian Jews to death by officially prohibiting the issuance of Orthodox baptismal certificates to Jews.

Serbian Orthodox Bishop Nikolaj Velimirovic, a revered leader of the Church, wrote:

> Europe is presently the main battlefield of the Jew and his father, the devil, against the heavenly Father and his only begotten Son…You should think about this, my Serbian brethren, and correspondingly correct your thoughts, desires and acts.[72]

Over ninety percent of Serbia's 16,000 Jews were exterminated and the Serbian Orthodox Church was complicit in their deaths.

The Serbian "heterodox" church wasn't the only party to Christian complicity. In Poland, during the 1930s, the Catholic Church embarked on a mission to shape a model of Polish nationalism that would be consistent with the Church's moral and political doctrine. Jews were a large ethnic minority of over three million and they posed a problem for the Church and for the political right wing, who viewed them as an economic and cultural threat, and detrimental to Polish national identity. August Hlond, the head of the Catholic Church in Poland, added his pious poison to the well of public sentiment in 1936 when he wrote a pastoral letter titled, "On the Principles of Catholic Morality." According to Hlond, "...the Jews do battle against the Church and serve as the vanguard of atheism and communism. Furthermore, they corrupt morality, disseminate pornography, and deal in treachery and usury."[73] Hlond's successor, Adam Sapieha, has been cited by sympathetic historians as having intervened on behalf of Polish Jews, but their grievous error of omission is that Sapieha and the Polish bishops intervened mostly on behalf of Catholics who were of Jewish origin. Three ecumenical councils were held by the Polish bishops during the occupation. None mentioned the mass murder of Jews. There were, however, a number of individual bishops and priests who were actively involved in helping

Jews by cooperating with an underground organization with ties to the ghetto and by hiding Jewish children in convents and monasteries.

In August, 1942, U.S. Secretary of State Cordell Hull was urging the Vatican to denounce Nazi atrocities against Jews, such as the liquidation of the Warsaw Ghetto and other mass murders. The Vatican flatly rejected American diplomatic efforts for any kind of papal intercession, writing to the American Ambassador to the Holy See: "…up to the present time it has not been possible to verify the accuracy thereof."[74]

But the "accuracy thereof" had been documented two months earlier. On June 25, 1942, the London *Daily Telegraph* wrote, "More than 700,000 Polish Jews have been slaughtered by the Germans in the greatest massacres in the world's history." The *Telegraph* headline on June 30 read, "More Than 1,000,000 Jews Killed in Europe." The BBC broadcast the stories and *The New York Times* carried the stories on June 30 and July 2. Radio stations all over Europe carried the stories. Three Jewish escapees gave detailed information about Polish death camps. But the Vatican, and the pope, remained silent, deafeningly silent.

Nine years earlier, on July 20, 1933, Cardinal Eugenio Pacelli, acting as the Vatican Secretary of State, signed a treaty with Adolf Hitler, the Reich Concordat. Hitler offered more funding for Catholic schools in Germany, while withdrawing educational benefits for Jews. In exchange, the obsequious Pacelli agreed to dissipate Germany's Catholic political groups, social associations and newspapers. He also agreed, as stated in Article 16 of the Concordat, to require Catholic bishops and priests to swear an oath of allegiance to the Third Reich. The Article read, in part:

> Before God and on the Holy Gospels I swear and promise...to honor the legally constituted Government and to cause the clergy of my diocese to honor it. In the performance of my spiritual office and in my solicitude for the welfare and the interests of the German Reich, I will endeavor to avoid all detrimental acts which might endanger it.

Hitler didn't want an organized Catholic presence in Germany, and Pacelli obliged. On signing the agreement, Hitler declared, "The concordant gives Germany an opportunity and creates an area of trust that is particularly significant in the developing struggle against international Jewry." Pacelli's Faustian bargain was construed by many as a tacit endorsement of Jewish persecution.

On March 12, 1939, Eugenio Pacelli was crowned Pope Pius XII. But the magisterium did not cure the muteness. When Hitler delivered a radio address, reprinted in Rome's *Messaggero* newspaper, declaring that "the Jews will be liquidated for at least a thousand years," there was heard not a peep from the pope.

The British minister to the Holy See, Francis D'Arcy Osborne pleaded with the pope to speak out. "His Holiness is clinging at all costs to what he considers to be a policy of neutrality, even in the face of the worst outrages against God and man."[75]

The "worst outrages against God and man" weren't known to many Jews in Europe. They were unaware of the fate awaiting them as they were deported to the death camps. But Pius XII was aware of the accounts of exterminations in the summer of 1942 when some fifteen thousand Dutch Jews were killed. He was aware of the protests of the Catholic bishops and Protestant churches of Holland sent to the German *Reichskommissar*. He was aware, but remained silent.

Even documents released by the Vatican confirm that he knew about the systematic killing of European Jews from 1942 on. Letters to him from bishops in early 1943 pleaded for the pope to speak out. A public protest would have saved lives.

In his influential castigation of Pius XII, Guenter Levy wrote:

A public denunciation of the mass murders by Pius XII, broadcast widely over the Vatican radio and read from the pulpits by the bishops, would have revealed to Jews and Christians alike what deportation to the East entailed. The pope would have been believed, whereas the broadcasts of the Allies were often shrugged off as war propaganda.[76]

When the pope appealed to the Allies not to bomb Rome, Osborne, the British minister, confided to his diary:

The more I think of it, the more I am revolted by Hitler's massacre of the Jewish race on the one hand, and, on the other, the Vatican's apparently exclusive preoccupation with the…possibilities of the bombardments of Rome.[77]

Osborne wrote to the Cardinal Secretary of State that the Vatican "…instead of thinking of nothing but the bombing of Rome should consider their duties in respect of the unprecedented crime against humanity of Hitler's campaign of extermination of the Jews."[78]

Scholars are in general agreement as to the less than divine inspiration for the pope's behavior. The man seemed preoccupied with protecting the church from communism. His immediate predecessor, Pius XI, vociferously condemned communism, and Pius XII echoed those sentiments. He believed that communism was inherently evil and a threat to his church. Historian Owen Chadwick wrote:

The new documents from the Vatican confirm once again the important role that the Vatican's interest in a strong Germany as a bulwark against Russian communism played in the development of a policy toward the Nazi regime…strict neutrality was one of the reasons that forbade a forthright condemnation of the murder of the Jews.[79]

One of Pacelli's concerns was that a protest would create a clash with Hitler that would benefit only the communists. His silence "…was no act of pusillanimity or fear of the Germans. He wanted to maintain the Nazi-occupation status quo…"[80]

While the pope played politics, six million Jews died. In stark contrast to the mute pope, Bishop Angelo Roncalli, who was in Bulgaria at the start of World War II, saved thousands of Hungarian, Bulgarian and Slovakian Jews. He urged his priests to issue false baptismal certificates, arranged to have orphaned children board refugee boats to Palestine, intervened at the Jasenovac and Sered concentration camps saving thousands of Jews, and performed many other acts of courage and compassion.

Many of the Catholic bishops in Slovakia had a contrarian attitude. The country was ruled by fascist dictator and priest Father Jozef Tiso, an anti-Semite whose regime became the first Nazi ally to agree to the deportation of Jews. The Catholic bishops issued a pastoral letter in 1942 in which they justified the persecution of Jews:

> The influence of the Jews [has] been pernicious. In a short time they have taken control of almost all the economic and financial life of the country. Not only economically, but also in the cultural and moral spheres, they have harmed our people. The Church cannot be opposed, therefore, if the state with legal regulations hinders the dangerous influence of the Jews.[81]

Tiso embraced anti-Jewish Nazi policies and enacted the Jewish Code which forbade Jews from owing real estate, participating in sports or cultural events or serving in public office. They were also excluded from secondary schools and universities and forced to wear the yellow star. After the end of the war, Tiso was tried, convicted and hanged for treason.

A few years after Tiso's reign of terror ended with him twisting slowly in the wind, Bishop Angelo Roncelli became a Cardinal and on November 4, 1958, was crowned Pope John XXIII. One of his first acts was to eliminate the description of Jews as "perfidious" in the Good Friday liturgy. He began an assertive policy of Christian-Jewish reconciliation generally acknowledged to have been among the best in the history of Christianity. He wrote of the Jewish people:

> We are conscious today that many, many centuries of blindness have cloaked our eyes so that we can no longer see the beauty of Thy chosen people nor recognize in their faces the features of our privileged brethren...Forgive us for the curse we falsely attached to their names as Jews. Forgive us...for we know not what we did.[82]

John XXIII became known as *"il Papa buono,"* "the good pope." He was declared a saint on April 27, 2014. The International Raoul Wallenberg Foundation has asked Yad Vashem to designate

Pope John XXIII as "Righteous Among the Nations."

No one has called for Pope Pius XII to be included among the righteous. The mute pope, time and time again, turned a deaf ear to the plight of the Jews. In September, 1942, President Roosevelt sent a personal representative, Myron Taylor, to plead with the pope to make a specific statement about the extermination of the Jews. The mission was fraught with danger, involving travel into enemy territory. Taylor presented the pope with copious documentation of German atrocities. He asked the pope to denounce not only the killing of Jews, but also the inhumane treatment of all refuges and hostages. Taylor encountered a shocking display of hypocrisy, arrogance and intransigence. The pope insisted that he *had* spoken out and that he deserved credit for his courageous actions. He said he would not make a distinction between the moralities of the combatants. He said he had shown a "feeling of pity and charity for the sufferings of civilians, for helpless women and children, for the sick and the aged…" He went on and on, but never once said the word "Nazi" or the word "Jew." He said nothing.

The efforts to beatify Pius XII have, not unexpectedly, met with vigorous resistance. The Catholic Church beatifies "...only those whose lives have been marked by the exercise of heroic virtue, and only after this has been proved by common repute for sanctity and by conclusive arguments."[83]

To arrive at a conclusive argument regarding this pope's "heroic virtue" would require distortions of history, denial of silence, and indefensible claims of saintly behavior. It would require deceitful revisionism and intellectual dishonesty by an entire church body. Garry Wills summarizes this steadfast unwillingness to face historical truth in his provocative book, *Papal Sin:*

> The debilitating effect of intellectual dishonesty can be touching. Even when papal authority sincerely wants to perform a virtuous act, when it spends years screwing up its nerve to do it, when it actually thinks it has done it, when it releases a notice of its having done it, when it expects to be congratulated on doing it – it has not done it. Not because it did not want to do it, or did not believe it

did it. It was simply unable to do it, because that would have involved coming clean about the record of the papal institution. And that is all but unthinkable.[84]

Elie Wiesel wrote, "The world knew and kept silent...Mankind let them suffer and agonize and perish alone. And yet, and yet they did not die alone, for something in all of us died with them."[85]

CHAPTER 3

Pathos

"For mercy has a human heart, pity a human face…"
William Blake

Those who showed compassion and pity toward Jews and other minorities during the Holocaust were indeed, the "righteous among nations." They risked their lives, and sacrificed their lives, to save people. Their motives were many and varied, but humane and life saving. These people made a decision, whether religious, moral or ethical, to do what they believed was the right thing to do.

Oskar Schindler was not known as a religious person, and according to No. 385 on Schindler's list, Victor Dortheimer, "…Schindler's motives for helping Jews were his sense of adventure and morality…He was always a little bit drunk and always with a beautiful woman. He was a gentleman gangster, but I think when he saw what was happening to the Jews he knew he had to help us."[86] Twenty years after the war, Schindler was asked why he behaved as he had. His answer was quite simple, "When you know people, you have to behave towards them like human beings..." [87] Schindler saved 1,100 Jews.

In 1949, a Nobel Prize for humanitarian efforts was awarded to the Quakers, for their active role in saving Jews during the Holocaust. Bertha Bracey, an English Quaker, played a prominent role in rescuing Jewish children in what became the Kindertransport. Scores of other groups and individuals demonstrated noble and humanitarian behavior that saved lives.

Dr. Nechama Tec, a Jewish Holocaust survivor and sociologist, was eight years old when her native Poland was invaded by the Germans. She has written extensively on the characteristics of rescuers and resisters and has challenged previous oversimplification of actions and motives. She analyzed courageous, altruistic behavior by the presence of several characteristics: individuality that approximates marginality, independence to act according to one's beliefs despite external pressures, long-standing commitment to aiding the helpless, perception of rescue as a necessary response to circumstances and not an act of heroism, unplanned initiation of rescue, and a universalistic view of Jews as needy human beings reliant on others' aid.[88]

But what about perpetrators? Did they feel compassion and pity toward their victims? Probably not. People and nations that have carried out the most evil acts of history did not regard their acts as evil, including those done with God's holy imprimatur. The Crusades and other papal-blessed Christian military campaigns against Muslims, Jews, witches, pagans and heretics lasted for hundreds of years. In the First Crusade, 8,000 Jews were killed in the Rhineland and 70,000 were slaughtered in the fall of Jerusalem. Historians consider that there were seven major Crusades between 1096 and 1291, plus numerous smaller military excursions. There is scant historical evidence that Crusaders felt guilt or shame for their actions.

While the undercurrents of Nazi genocide were more social and political than religious, the lack of compassion and mercy for the victims was the same as in previous genocides. Those who may have felt any pangs of guilt came up with preposterous rationalizations during and after the war. And what should we think of those who merely stood by, did nothing and said nothing? Pleadings of innocence by indifferent civilians were twisted and implausible. But were they evil? Elie Wiesel implored:

> Don't be indifferent…indifference is now equal to evil. And I have always felt that the opposite of culture is not ignorance; it is indifference. And the opposite of faith is not atheism; again, it's indifference. And the opposite of morality is not immorality; it's again indifference.[89]

Those who did nothing were not innocent. They felt no shared humanity with their Jewish neighbors, nor did they feel any instinctive altruism or predisposition for goodness or kindness. Their motionless inertia served as Hitler's handmaiden, and death diminished their humanity. The hackneyed cliché attributed to Edmund Burke sums it up: "The only thing necessary for the triumph of evil is for good men to do nothing." Equally poignant and prescient is this call to action from Burke: "When bad men combine, the good must associate; else they will fall, one by one, an unpitied sacrifice in a contemptible struggle."[90]

Psychiatrists think it's the absence of morals that let some people commit crimes. They use terms like "psychopath," "sociopath" and "antisocial personality" to describe these people. Beware of psychopaths, we are warned, because they are especially dangerous as they lack any form of conscience. Some can commit a crime and pass a polygraph test. They have no sense of guilt or shame. We often call these people evil, but to many doctors of the mind and behavior, that is a flawed, imprecise concept. One useful definition by a prominent psychologist considers evil as "...passionate destructiveness, justified by righteousness and expressed with little inhibition and with ruthless disregard for consequences."[91]

This ruthless disregard was evident and obvious in the behavior of Nazi soldiers and officers. For humans to act this way was abhorrent. For Nazi doctors to act this way was an incomprehensible paradox. These were doctors who had sworn an oath to protect human life. The

Nazi euthanasia program began even before the war when German doctors were recruited to kill people who were mentally retarded or who had other handicaps, conditions and illnesses. Decisions were made as to whose life was worth living and whose was not. The pre-war killing program would provide useful techniques and procedures to use later in the mass murder of Jews and other victims.

◆ ◆ ◆

As a university student in Munich, Dimitrios studied law and philosophy, but gravitated toward theology, which interested him more. Wrestling with the cumbersome problem of evil, he found the early philosophers' thoughts on religion edifying, but unsatisfying. Plato's *Republic* had assigned evil acts to the misuse of free will. But reconciling acts of evil with the goodness of God was not easy for the young student. Later thinkers, such as Thomas Aquinas and René Descartes, did not help. Aquinas taught that man was naturally self-determined to the good and that evil choices were simply the will's attempt to satisfy mistaken, spurious desires that alienated the soul from God. Descartes also believed that man was naturally inclined to follow the good, that his will, behavior and reason were naturally directed toward the truth. But the inventor of analytical geometry could not come up with a formula for the reconciliation riddle. Reconciling human free will with divine foreordination was too deep a mystery, too complicated to fathom. It was insoluble.

For Dimitrios, the inquisitive bishop-to-be, the mysterious, unfathomable idea of evil remained irreconcilable with the "ineffable, incomprehensible, invisible, inconceivable" God of the Orthodox Church. His comic solace lay in the spacial paradox of the Stoic Zeno, whose Achilles could never overtake the tortoise in a race because he would always have half the distance to travel to catch up with the tortoise. And that was how Dimitrios felt. There were some truths that were unreachable, unknowable. You just couldn't get there. They remained a mystery. The human free will that exerted its evil on Zakynthos forty years later would be an insoluble mystery, and a horrifying reality.

◆　◆　◆

In 1943, American psychologist Abraham Maslow published a paper, "A Theory of Human Needs," in which he outlined a hierarchy of needs. He listed "belongingness" as the third level of human needs after physiological and safety needs. The theory was that humans want to feel a sense of belonging and acceptance among their social groups. In Germany, this sense of belonging developed with a ferocious intensity, hastening a collective identity across all strata of German society. This identity soon transmogrified into a collective narcissism, a state of mind in which the individual had an inflated self-love of the "in-group," and a concomitant hatred of others. This group-think spawned an evil gang of perpetrators, "...human subjects who, by their own decision, dehumanized other subjects and, in doing so, did not only pervert the sovereign subjectivity of the victims but challenged also their own sacredness."[92]

The prescient French philosopher and novelist Julien Benda presented a similar point of view in 1928. He wrote of the racial, class and national passions that caused men to rise up against other men and how these passions made an individual feel part of something much larger, something much more meaningful and glorious. The common political/social attitudes toward Jews in Germany impassioned a mass of people to form a collective identity, bestowing on the individual "...a mystic personality on the association of which he feels himself a member, and gives it a religious adoration, which is simply the deification of his own passion, and no small stimulus to its intensity." [93] With prophetic accuracy, Benda analyzed the prevailing emotional, political and ideological undercurrents in Germany, which eventually erupted in World War II. He knew with certainty that these troubled waters would be noted in history:

> Our age is indeed the age of the intellectual organization of political hatreds. It will be one of its chief claims to notice in the moral history of humanity. [94]

Historians, theologians and social scientists believe that the Nazis did not regard what they did as evil. Germans felt victimized and outraged after World War I and Hitler used this to gain power.

The murderous atrocities of the Third Reich were facilitated by political and psychological factors, including the decline of individual responsibility. Soldiers were "just taking orders" and German citizens claimed no knowledge of the atrocities. During the post-war trials, responsibility for one's actions was seldom expressed. Murderous behavior was not criminal and thus there was no guilt, no shame, no regret. Nazi General Wilhelm Keitel said at his trial:

> I did not have any inner conviction of becoming criminal...since after all it was the head of the state who, as far as we were concerned, held all the legislative power. Consequently, I did not consider that I was acting criminally. I took part in the murder of many people. I often asked myself after the war whether I had become a criminal...and found no answer.[95]

Ordinary people obeying orders, the "banality of evil" as Hannah Arendt called it, was a social pathology. It allowed Nazi soldiers and German citizens to conform to mass opinion without considering the consequences of their actions, or inactions. It allowed the individual to follow the Führer without following his or her conscience. It allowed premeditated genocide.

In her book on the Eichmann trial, Deborah Lipstadt wrote that individual Nazis were not transformed from ordinary men to murderers in some random fashion, but instead "...traversed a path paved by centuries of pervasive anti-Semitism. They 'knew' this road and, given the society in which they lived, it seemed true and natural."[96]

Asher Moissis, one of the most incisive and prolific Jewish writers in modern Greece, delivered a powerful, chastising speech in Athens following the liberation in October, 1944. He said, in part:

> The Germans could perhaps claim after their conclusive defeat, demanding to be believed, that World War II was provoked by Hitler's oligarchy without a mandate from or the approval of the German people...No German, however, will have the audacity to want to confine the responsibility for the crimes against the Jewish people to a narrow circle of supporters of Hitler's party or of Prussian

militarism, because Hitler's entire anti-Jewish extermination plan in its full extent and with all its detail was publicly proclaimed as the political program of Hitler's party, and the German people approved this program by means of free elections and by a large majority, bringing Hitler and his party to power. The legal liability therefore of the entire German people for all the bad and horrible acts committed against us is obvious and self-evident.[97]

That was his legal and political castigation (Moissis was a respected lawyer). He also spoke of the "inalienable ideological property of the entire German people" which included a variety of Nazi manifestations besides anti-Semitism – imperialism, the desire to overthrow international order, the repudiation of international law, the tendency to enslave people, the enslavement of the power of the spirit to the violent state, and the subjugation of the biblical ideal of universal love and brotherhood.[98]

In a public resolution on the day after the liberation, Moissis expressed his gratitude to the people of Greece:

Miracle at Zakynthos

> We the Israelites...declare publicly and
> before all free mankind our feelings of
> profound gratitude that we and our
> descendants will carry toward the Greek
> people in their entirety, who by all kinds
> of moral and material support and
> assistance made our rescue possible.[99]

Greece was also indebted to its Jewish citizens who had a history of serving in the nation's armed forces. In the 1897 war between Greece and Turkey, Jews from Zakynthos, Corfu, Patras, Athens and Chalkis fought in the Greek army. Greek Jews also served in the Balkan Wars in 1912-1923, the First World War, Greece's campaign in Asia Minor in 1919-1923, the War with Italy in 1940-1941, and of course, World War II. In 1913, King Constantine praised the Jewish fighters:

> Israelite soldiers fought in the Greek army
> as patriots, oftentimes as heroes...This
> constitutes clear proof of sincere and true
> patriotism.[100]

One of the greatest military heroes in the war against Italy was a Jewish colonel, Mordechai Frizis, who had joined the army as a volunteer. He was the only Greek army colonel killed in combat during that war. He was honored with the Greek Gold Medal for Bravery and today there are over two dozens streets in Greece that bear his name.

◆ ◆ ◆

A cocktail of strong idealism with a dash of delusional utopian fantasy can be toxic. That was the German Kool-Aid at the start of World War II. People who committed vicious acts of brutality did not believe they were doing evil things. They believed they were doing good. They thought they were making the world a better place, and getting even for past injustices. They believed that concentration camps were for relocating people, not for killing them.

There was no "banality of evil" associated with Hitler's madness. His sanity has been difficult to diagnose by historians and biographers, but it is generally agreed that he was a hypochondriac, suffered from psychosomatic illnesses, was depressed, compulsive, paranoid and psychopathic.

In 1940, Hitler came up with a plan to build a new institute in Frankfurt to educate the German people about the Jews. He chose Alfred Rosenberg, a leading Nazi ideologue, to seize all Jewish cultural, scientific and archival materials for the new institute. Rosenberg was one of the main authors of Nazi ideological creeds, including its racial theory, persecution of the Jews and opposition to "degenerate and subversive" modern art (Klee, Kandinsky, Chagall, Matisse).

In April, 1941, the Rosenberg Sonderkommandos, a unit of about thirty German officers and academics, scoured the country, invading synagogues, associations, schools, banks, newspapers, bookshops, hospitals and private homes. Their cruel and brazen actions resulted in the plunder of tens of thousands of archives, synagogue ornaments and priceless collections of books, manuscripts, artworks, rabbinical judgments and personal possessions. At Nuremberg, Rosenberg was sentenced to death and hanged as a war criminal and for crimes against humanity.

Hitler's obsession with Jews remains a mystery, but theories abound. He hated his cruel and abusive father Alois, and believed his paternal grandfather was Jewish. To prevent people like his evil father from ever being born again, he prohibited Jews from marrying or having sex with Aryans.

The cruelty Alois heaped upon his son is what psychotherapists claim caused Adolf's self-loathing and craving for revenge, and tormented his mind with the repulsive thought that there was Jewish blood in his veins and that he himself had been a victim of Jews.

There is controversy among Hitler's biographers as to the Jewish grandfather, but many believe that Hitler felt he had been poisoned by Jewish blood. "The phantom Jew may never have existed, but in Adolf's mind he was a powerful figure, standing behind the morbid obsession that drove him to bleed himself with leeches and, after he identified himself with Germany, to bleed the nation."[101]

While studying in Munich, Dimitrios met young Adolf, an aspiring artist. What struck Dimitrios was that there were no people in any of Adolf's paintings.

CHAPTER 4

OCCUPATION

"These people saved us. They were very special."

Lilly Arouch

On April 27, 1941, Bishop Chrysostomos learned from his radio that the Germans had entered the city of Athens. The mayor, Ambrosios Plitas, solemnly announced that he and other mayors along with high-ranking military officers met with the Germans and surrendered the city. At 10:30 a.m., the Greek flag at the Acropolis was lowered and replaced by the German flag. About a dozen German soldiers, acting like exuberant tourists, posed for a photo in front of the Parthenon.

Several weeks after the Germans occupied Athens, two college students, Manolis Glezos and Apostolos Santas, committed a brazen act of symbolic resistance. Under cover of night, they climbed the northwest face of the Acropolis and tore down the large Nazi swastika flag. This heroic act served to galvanize the resistance movement throughout the country. Other acts of resistance and sabotage, less symbolic and more deadly, proliferated all across Greece, including Zakynthos. The Germans responded with grossly inordinate retaliation, burning villages and killing civilians.

On the eastern front, armed bands committed acts of sabotage against the Germans resulting in a policy of harsh retaliation, and on September 20, 1941, orders were issued dealing with the suppression of insurgency in occupied Europe. The order stated that for any attack on or death of a German soldier, between fifty to one hundred hostages were to be shot. In Greece, the order specifically stated that fifty Greeks would be killed for every German death.[102] The Germans did not always follow the order however. When a German police captain was killed in the town of Cumi, fifty Greeks were executed, but when the *andartes* attacked a truck convoy of German uniformed police in Salonika, sixty hostages were killed in reprisal, and when a German officer, General Krech, was killed in an ambush, two hundred people were massacred. The reprisals were effective in spreading terror in the towns and villages, but did little to diminish the resistance efforts. As historian John Louis Hondros explains:

> The order assumed that…only severe retaliation could halt the spread of resistance…the Germans shot first and asked questions later…this indiscriminate policy of reprisals did not slow down the growth of the resistance movements…but only intensified the struggle and alienated the population.[103]

Concurrent with the murderous reprisals, the Germans tried conciliatory initiatives, such as endowing two chairs in German language and literature at the University of Athens, which had been closed during the occupation. The Greek students showed their appreciation for the new chairs by staging angry protests and demonstrations against the Germans and the quisling government. The University was shut down the very next day after it had opened.

Chrysostomos wondered which of the occupying forces would take command of the Ionian Islands. He learned within hours that Cephalonia to the north had been invaded by the

Italians. Four days later, on a sunny spring morning, three Italian officers and about a hundred Italian soldiers landed on Zakynthos. In the name of King Victor Emmanuel, they took over the island.

A curfew was set from nine in the evening to five in the morning. A proclamation was issued that stated, in part:

> The people of the Ionian Islands are now under the flag of Italy and the red, green and white banner flies over the islands. This is a great gift and if the islanders accept Italy, they will have peace and justice.

"Peace and justice" included a fine on all non-Italians to support the Italian military, the confiscation of all motor vehicles, the pillaging of stores and homes, the confiscation of food supplies, and the occasional brutality.

The famine on the mainland did not spare the islands. Chrysostomos immediately began a dialogue with the Italian military on Zakynthos and the Italian headquarters in Corfu. His people were starving and needed food. On June 15, 1941,

Chrysostomos met with a small group of patriots to organize a resistance movement with a clandestine headquarters and hidden radio. Feeding people was an immediate priority and the group went to work. Two of the resistance members attempting to smuggle food from Cephalonia were caught by the Italians and shot to death. The Italians suspected the bishop was involved but could find no direct evidence. They issued harsh orders to slow the resistance movement: no one was allowed to come onto the island without permission and there would be harsh reprisals for black market activity.

The bishop continued his protests until the Italians relented and created spectacles of bread giving in the main square. An Italian fascist band played raucous military music while the poor and starving stood in long lines for morsels of bread. Children found these cacophonous grotesqueries amusing.

Since the Italians could not find and capture members of the resistance movement, they started arresting heads of organizations that were distributing food and supplies to the citizens of Zakynthos. They were charged with sabotage and jailed. The bishop was told that since all goods on the island belonged to the Italians, these organizations had no right to distribute grapes, olives, fruits, nuts, cheese or anything else. The bishop was able to get many of these people released.

The Italians continued arresting people. Now it was teachers and professionals, jailed on trumped up charges of collaborating with the British or being communists. Chrysostomos announced to the local military commander that unless these people were released, he would join them in jail. Communication was sent to Mussolini and the prisoners were released.

◆ ◆ ◆

In ancient Greece, kings and athletes were anointed with olive oil. The sacred lamps of the temples burned olive oil for illumination, and the eternal flame of the original Olympics used olive oil. On Zakynthos, the olive trees were hundreds of years old. Based on scientific verification and archaeological evidence, a tree on Crete (the Finix Olive) was estimated to be nearly 2,000 years old. The trunks of these trees are broad, gnarled and very hardy. They are asymmetrical and somewhat surreal, as if imagined by Hieronymus Bosch. On Zakynthos during the occupation, the olive trees were a mainstay of the island's economy and were regarded with a reverence accorded to ancient things and people.

Chrysostomos came running when he heard the church bells. He saw people rushing from their homes and shops, heading toward an olive grove several kilometers outside the town. Unbeknownst to them, Zakynthos was going to become an Axis air force base for the landing of Italian planes on the way from Africa to Italy, and on that day, the Italians began destroying olive trees to build a landing strip. The sight was sickening – dozens of ancient olive trees set ablaze, sacrificing food of life for products of war. This Greek tragedy was met with a chorus of anguished cries and damning curses. For the first time since the occupation, the bishop felt helpless. The following day, he tried to stop the Italians from confiscating property and destroying homes to make way for the landing strip, but was told this was necessary in order to bring in military vehicles, tractors and heavy equipment.

When they weren't working or confiscating food, the Italians were often seen playing football (soccer) in the town square. One Sunday morning, a group of soldiers damaged a statue of the national poet (Dionysios Solomos) in Plateia Solomou. When confronted by an angry group of Greeks, the Italians falsely blamed the damage on local citizens, claiming that the statue had been damaged the day before. The confrontation escalated with threats and accusations of sabotage. The Italians, at gunpoint, ordered the crowd to disperse and threatened to execute ten Greeks. A delegation led by Chrysostomos ran to see the Italian commander. The bishop pleaded with him, insisting that innocent people should not be killed, regardless who was at fault for the damaged statue. Instead of executions, the Italians levied a fine on the islanders (100 drachmas per person) as punishment.[104] Adding insult to injury, the name Plateia Solomou was changed to Plateia Mussolini. All major squares and streets had their names changed as well.

The Italians took over the public schools and changed the curricula to reflect "Italianizing" of the children. Orders were issued requiring all children between the ages of seven and twelve to report for baths, special uniforms and instruction on becoming good fascists. They were told to report every morning at 7:00 to receive indoctrination.[105]

Mussolini began issuing a number of orders designed to incorporate Zakynthos and all the Ionian islands as a part of Italy, subject to Italian law, customs and traditions. The absurdity and arrogance of these orders strengthened the resolve of the resistance on the islands. As he studied the detailed orders affecting the Greek islands, the bishop found nothing in particular relating to the Jewish population. Tragically, this would change under the German occupation.

The bishop's provocations were annoying the Italians. During the 1942 New Year celebration at the church of St. Dionysios, the bishop addressed the congregation with hope and enthusiasm:

> Be patient my beloved. We are Greeks and we will win. The occupiers will leave the island. Zakynthos is Greek and will always be Greek.[106]

Word got back to the Italian commander on the island, Luigi Gianni, that the bishop was using his pulpit as a weapon of propaganda. Gianni came to the service the following week and heard the bishop ask God to protect the Greek people and to free the island from oppression. Gianni confronted the bishop after the service and threatened him, demanding that he stop preaching and inciting his parishioners. The bishop told Gianni that he was not fearful for his own safety, that his only concern was for his flock, and that he would stop speaking out only when his voice was silenced. Two months later, on March 25 (Greek Independence Day), the bishop spoke passionately about the glorious history of Greeks fighting off conquerors and the need to follow in that tradition. During Good Friday services on April 3, he likened the current plight to Golgotha. Gianni had enough. He conferred with the Italian Head of the Ionian Islands, Piero Parini, and they devised a strategy to deal with the bishop. They would use food to satisfy his hunger and soften his rhetoric. But their first foray was rebuffed when a cartload of bread sent to the bishop was returned with a note thanking the Italians but stating that he would suffer hunger along with his flock.

For the bishop, the handwriting was on the wall. Konstantino Katsoura, a magistrate and war hero from the Albanian front, was ordered along with his family to leave the island as punishment for his lack of respect for the Italian fascists. Members of the legal profession were arrested and held as hostages until the Italians could find and arrest resistance fighters. On December 12, 1942, under cover of night, the hostages were put on a boat and taken away, never to be seen again. Other arrests followed, targeting bankers, merchants, teachers, clergy, writers and poets. The bishop knew his days were numbered.

On February 1, 1943, Chrysostomos was charged with treason, shackled and imprisoned in the fortress. Ten days later, he was exiled to a prison in Athens, where he remained until his release in November.

The propaganda coming from the Italian radio program, Il Voce, painted a rosy picture of Italian successes, but the hidden radio belonging to the guerilla resistance told the real story – the Italians were losing ground and the islanders celebrated the defeats in Africa, the invasion of Sicily, the air raid on Rome and the fall of Mussolini.

Along with radio broadcasts came divine intervention. The Italians went to the highest peak on the island to set up anti-aircraft guns to shoot down British planes. They chose an Orthodox church, Prophet Elias, to position their guns. When the first British plane was sighted, the Italians started firing. Apparently, the vibrations from the weapons caused the old church ceiling and walls to shake, crumble and fall, killing the Italian gunners and burying them under a mass of consecrated rubble. The islanders considered this a miracle from God, an apt and auspicious metaphor for the failing Italian war effort and impending demise of the Italian colonial empire.

On May 21, 1943, the Germans arrived on Zakynthos, disarmed the Italians and sent them to Cephalonia, where 1,646 Italian soldiers were summarily shot and killed. On September 8, General Dwight Eisenhower publicly announced the surrender of Italy to the Allies. The Germans accused the Italians of treason and blamed it on the Jews. German radio broadcasters were furious and hysterical:

With this, a veil has been torn from a treacherous intrigue which for weeks had been enacted by an Italian clique, serfs to Jews and alien to their own people.[107]

One week after the Italian surrender, the Germans launched a brutal attack against the remaining Italian troops on Cephalonia. Four thousand Italians were killed, and over 40,000 were made prisoners of war or deported to the eastern front for forced labor, as per Hitler's orders.[108]

◆　◆　◆

Captain Alfredo Litt was placed in charge of the German occupation forces on Zakynthos. Litt was cruel and efficient and prepared to follow orders, like the ones Hitler issued regarding the Italian massacre on the other Ionian islands. Litt often added emphasis to his commands with the barrel of his 9mm Luger. A young Greek Jew, Raphael Constantinos, recalled a terrifying encounter with the new commander:

I made tin cups with my dad. The Germans lived above our place. One day

the commander came in and pointed his
gun at me because his cups weren't ready.
He didn't know we were Jews and the
Greeks didn't tell on us.[109]

New, more restrictive curfews were enacted
by the Germans. On the first day of the occupation,
a young Greek villager, unaware of the new
curfew, was shot and killed by a German officer.
Litt ordered that his body be left in the street for
twenty-four hours as an example.

The atrocities continued. Citizens were
arrested for minor infractions. Every day, young
Greek men were rounded up for forced labor. Their
only meal consisted of an afternoon serving of
horta (steamed greens) and water but no bread.
Shlomo Amar remembered the day his father,
Moshe, was taken to a camp where men were
forced to remove large stones and move soil to
make roads for German vehicles. The Germans
noticed the box of tools the tinsmith (many Jews on
the island were tinsmiths and blacksmiths) carried
with him and put him to work making cans which
were sent back to Germany. Most of the men at the
camp knew Moshe was Jewish, but didn't say a

word. One of the men, while being questioned by the Germans, said, "We don't have any Jews, just Greeks here."[110] Many of the men died from the hardship, the beatings or from exposure to the harsh winter of 1943—1944. Random public executions became commonplace.

The atrocities strengthened the resolve of the resistance groups. More and more young men and women, and a number of older people headed into the remote mountains to join the guerillas.

A Greek government memo, obviously not from the collaborationists, was sent in October, 1943 to the German authorities regarding the Jews in Greece:

> Jews have become one with the Greek people. They have produced many poets and have repeatedly distinguished themselves on the field of battle.

> They have distinguished themselves in military and judicial matters, and have handled delicate matters most conscientiously. Greek history ignores anti-Semitism and intends doing so now.

The Greek Orthodox Church has always given protection to the Jewish minority, which is small in numbers and offers no racial or political obstacle.

The nature of the Greek people refuses to distinguish people by their races, and judges them only as individuals according to the teachings of the ancient and modern Greek intellectual world.[111]

Memoranda, nor any other protestation, could not attenuate the intensity of Nazi hatred of Jews. On Zakynthos, as well as in towns and cities throughout Greece, the order was given to place a Star of David on the door of every Jewish home, an order many Jewish families chose to ignore, especially since many had false Christian ID papers. Some Jews moved in with Christian families, mindful of the warning that any Greek Christian caught hiding or helping a Jew would be shot and their house burned to the ground. Shlomo Amar remembered the gruesome sight of a man hung from an olive tree because the Germans suspected him of giving food to a poor Jewish family. The Germans often forbade the family of a murdered person to retrieve the hung body, which after time, became bloated and burst, spreading deadly and contagious typhus. "My younger brother got sick and nearly died from the typhus,"[112] recalled Shlomo.

Newspapers in Tel Aviv published lengthy reports on German atrocities. They also ran stories about those who risked their lives to protect and save Jews. Regarding Greeks, the daily paper *Hasman* wrote:

> The Jewish people all over the world notes with the greatest satisfaction this conduct on the part of the heroic sons of Greece, whose spiritual values continue always to set an example of civilization and humanity.[113]

A group of Greek Jewish refugees arrived in Syria and gave this account to the daily Tel Aviv newspaper *Haaretz:*

> We owe a perpetual debt of gratitude to the Greek patriots who saved us and fed us, endangering their own lives. The Greek captain of the small boat which

brought us refused to take money for our passage, and he distributed among us the best of whatever he had.[114]

A correspondent for the Tel Aviv daily, *Davar*, sent a telegram stating, in part, "[t]he Jews are full of gratitude to the Greek people for the generosity and nobility of their feelings. Such fraternity among fellow-citizens had never before been reported in history."[115]

The Chief Rabbi of Palestine, Yitzhak Herzog, made this proclamation at a religious conference:

The Jewish Palestinian people, and, with them, the Jewish people of the United States, of Britain and of the entire world, would like to express their heartfelt thanks to the Greek Orthodox Church, and, in particular, that of occupied Greece, for the moral and material assistance it has given to the persecuted Jews, and also for the understanding which the worthy leaders of that Church have displayed towards the sufferings and problems now concerning the Jewish people.[116]

While in prison, Bishop Chrysostomosheard stories from the world press, the Red Cross and from other prisoners about the mass deportation of European Jews. And his suspicions were confirmed; deportations had begun in Greece. He was shocked to hear that the final destination for most Greek Jews was Auschwitz-Birkenau, where the inherent characteristics of their Greek Jewry worked against them. For example, "Greek Jews could not speak the languages of the camp: Yiddish, Polish and German, a fact that further hampered their ability to survive. Orders must be executed immediately; the inability to comprehend could mean instant death."[117]

The survival statistics at Auschwitz-Birkenau were grim. According to the Central Board of Jewish Communities and Yad Vashem, a total of over 55,000 Greek Jews were sent to Auschwitz-Birkenau. Of those, 42,509 (nearly 80%) were sent to their deaths immediately; 12,948 were put into forced labor. Fewer than 2,000 survived.

There were numerous acts of suicide in the death camps, but there was one collective act that was unique in the history of Auschwitz. A group of about 400 Greek Jews was selected to join a dead body disposal unit. Their duties were explained to them and they were ordered to begin disposing of bodies. The men held a secret meeting and announced their collective refusal to follow the order. Dr. Josef Mengele was outraged and threatened them with death. They again refused and were immediately gassed. A Hungarian nurse in the women's camp, Olga Lengyel, first reported the incident in her postwar memoir: "...what a demonstration of courage and character these Greek peasants had given. A pity the world does not know more about them."[118]

Most of the world does not know about another historic event -- the only revolt in the history of Auschwitz. It took place on October 7, 1944. Several Jewish women who worked in the munitions factory were smuggling small quantities of dynamite and some weapons into the crematoria. The plan was to stage a camp revolt, but under the circumstances, it was difficult to synchronize their activities, so the revolt began ahead of schedule. There were about four hundred prisoners involved, divided into four squads -- two were comprised of Greek Jews and the other two included French and Hungarian Jews plus a contingent of nineteen Russian Jewish soldiers. Two of the squads lost their courage and backed out at the last minute. The remaining two squads, comprised of 135 Greek Jews, did not. A signal was given and they rushed the guards and blew up the furnaces and smokestacks of two crematoria before they were killed. According to survivor testimony, some twenty German guards were killed, one crematorium was completely destroyed and another extensively damaged. [119] These heroic actions reduced the killing capacity of the crematoria by half and raised the morale of the prisoners. It was reported that "in the rubble of crematorium III, the Greek Jews died singing the Greek national anthem."[120]

There were few escapes from Auschwitz. Most prisoners who made it outside the camp were tracked down and shot. Hella Kounio and five others were among those few who escaped and survived:

> We were five girls from Greece: my daughter, myself and three others...I told the others that we should steal something from the storage rooms and escape into

the woods. When we left the other inmates to escape into the woods we were wearing gray clothes with white scarves on our heads...I remember it as if it happened yesterday. We saw that the soldiers were beginning to break rank, so we figured we'd run away ourselves—what worse could happen to us?...We walked for six days until we reached a hill on top of which we saw many people. There was a building from which men were coming out of. We didn't know who they were, so we kept away that night and slept nearby. The morning after, we saw soldiers. They were not Germans—they had British and French uniforms on, so I approached them. Former prisoners of war, they were Americans, British, French and Yugoslavs...From there we were told to move on to the British zone...On our way there, we saw a forest of oak trees, with green and very beautiful leaves...Under every tree there was a concentration camp inmate, face on the ground, with a bullet hole on the back of the head. Erika and I turned each of the bodies around to see if my husband and son were among them. We didn't find them.[121]

Hella's husband and two children survived and the family returned to Greece after the war's end. But 1.5 million other children did not survive. A Greek Jewish Auschwitz survivor, Sam Profetas, recalled a scene of great anguish at the camp:

> In one of those new transports that were constantly arriving, I saw a mother holding a baby in her arms and holding another child by the hand. The older child asked, "Mom, where are they taking us?" She answered, "First we will take a bath, and then we will meet dad, grandpa, grandma, and the others." I then lifted my eyes towards the sky and started begging God, saying, "My God, maybe we grownups are at fault for something and you condemn us, but do make a miracle happen for these children." I even begged Christ…as well as all the Gods of every religion I know of, even Buddha, to at least save the children. And I said that if, by any chance, I were to come out of there alive I would dedicate my life to the children.[122]

As the Russians were closing in on Auschwitz, the Germans forced Profetas and other prisoners to march for two days in freezing temperatures to Gleivitz and then put them on cattle cars which took them to Gusen II in Austria, part of the Mauthausen concentration camp. On May 5, 1945, American troops liberated the camp.

> When the Americans came and collected the corpses, they thought I was dead too. But they saw that I still had a pulse and discovered I was alive....I weighed, as they later told me, 28 kilograms.[123]

Profetas returned to Greece after the war's end and did, in fact, dedicate his life to helping children in Salonika, working at the Jewish community center, kindergarten and summer camp for many years.[124]

❖   ❖   ❖

There were nearly 60,000 Jews living in Salonika in northern Greece, the most populous city of Sephardic Jews in the world for over 400 years. Jews were confined to the ghetto and their movement severely restricted. On December 6, 1942 the Germans began to dismantle the Jewish cemetery where they uprooted an estimated hundred thousand tombstones. Skeletal remains were strewn across the area as German soldiers picked through the bones looking for gold teeth, jewelry and anything else of value.[125] Jewish men were publicly humiliated, beaten and forced to work in mines and quarries, on roads and building airports. Many died from tuberculosis, typhus, malaria and dysentery.[126]

The Chief Rabbi, Zevi Koretz, announced from the pulpit of the Beth Saoul Synagogue, that his congregation should obey the German orders, assuring everyone that the German authorities had pledged their word and could be trusted to issue no further measures against them. On March 5, 1943, he issued the following appeal:

> We appeal to all our coreligionists to maintain their calmness and self-discipline. We ask them not to panic and to believe in rumors, which are all baseless. Everyone should continue his work and should have confidence in the leaders of the community.[127]

Angel Mirou-Mairy listened to the rabbi's appeal but felt he was giving bad advice. At twenty-two and the oldest of six children, she refused to acquiesce.

> The rabbi came and told us we had to wear a yellow star. All the Jews had to wear it in order to be distinguished from others. But for me there was no yellow star. I took it off and went wherever I wanted…The rabbi was responsible for what happened. He came and told us that there was nothing to worry about. He advised us to give all our assets to the Germans and go work for them. He lied to us.[128]

Angel and her family got Christian IDs, changed their last name and went into hiding until the war's end.

Dr. George Karakotsios was a prominent tuberculosis doctor in Salonika. He and his wife Fedra knew that their Jewish friends and neighbors, the Arouch family, were in danger. The doctor insisted that the family of five move in with them. Lilly Arouch, the oldest of three girls, vividly and fondly recalled the family that saved them:

These people saved us, they were very special. They had an eight-year-old boy then. These people took us in, gave us their room and hid us there for nineteen months. They shared with us the little bread and food they had, and also our fear and frustration. It was a very hard time for us, and for them. We were all very scared. Imagine, we were living in a very small apartment and every sound and every knock on the door was scary for us. My father was hiding in a closet and my mother was hiding under a bed.[129]

While many fearful Jews went into hiding, Rabbi Koretz became a servile organ of the Germans. They gave orders and he followed them. He refused any attempt by resistance fighters to help the Jews. EAM and other resistance groups pleaded with the Jews to ignore German orders and leave the city, but Koretz rebuffed them, galvanizing his people with assurances of safety. Meanwhile, he handed over to the Rosenberg Gestapo Battalion all the registers of the Jewish community. In return, the Gestapo commandeered a two-story building and gave it to Koretz to use as his office. They also gave him two motor vehicles, an eight-seater and a five-seater taxi.

On March 14, 1943, the Germans ordered Rabbi Koretz to address his congregation and announce their imminent deportation to Krakow. He assured his tearful people that the great community of Krakow (not aware that it had been destroyed), "will look after our settlement there. Every one of us will find work according to his desire, ability, knowledge and experience."[130]

The next day, the transports of Jews from Salonika began. The Jewish people who trusted Rabbi Koretz realized their mistake. They condemned him and other Jewish leaders for their willingness to comply with the German orders, for their failure to understand and anticipate German intentions, and for discouraging any resistance and escape. When an overflow crowd confronted him at the synagogue of Monastirioton, the rabbi had the audacity to tell them, "The times are tragic and difficult. Have patience and courage."[131]

Koretz had a weak and servile character, the perfect type to be selected as a collaborator. Before the transports had begun, the Germans decided to test the rabbi's character and physical resistance.

They called him at two o'clock in the morning and ordered him to deliver a donkey before sunrise. A terrified Koretz frantically called people asking for a donkey, which he found and delivered at daybreak to the German officers, who knew they had found their man.

In a liberation speech reflecting on the fate of his fellow citizens, the Jewish lawyer and writer, Asher Moissis said:

> Salonika, the mother city of Israel. There our poor brothers, psychologically unprepared, lacking direction, and misled by a corrupt and blameworthy communal leadership, were suddenly caught in the Himmlerian trap and kidnapped, almost in their totality, under conditions indescribable and horrific, as slaves in foreign and unknown countries, where every care and attention was taken for their fate to remain completely unknown to us.[132]

The complicity of Koretz was a sharp contrast to the courageous actions of other rabbis, most notably Chief Rabbi Elias Barzilai of Athens who refused German orders, risked his life saving Jewish citizens and joined the resistance fighters.

As the transports continued, Rabbi Koretz was no longer useful to the Germans. He was arrested, imprisoned and then deported with his family to Bergen-Belsen where he was forced to do hard labor, eventually caught typhus and died three months after the liberation by the Russians. Seventy years later, his role still remains a contentious issue, with some Salonika Holocaust scholars believing that he was guilty of naiveté rather than collaboration,[133] while others, such as Asher Moissis, found him more culpable:

> Koretz undoubtedly did not seek the annihilation of the Jews of Salonika, but by finding himself at the head of this great community, he had the duty either to sacrifice himself for them or to set the example of resistance, either passive or active.[134]

The Italians opposed the deportations and issued formal diplomatic protests which were ignored. The Germans planned to deport ten thousand Jews per week with as many as sixty people packed into each cattle car. Again, the Italians tried unsuccessfully to intervene, suggesting that the Jews could be relocated and concentrated on one of the Greek islands instead. For most Italians, the systematic extermination of an entire people was grotesque and unacceptable. The final solution was an abhorrent way of thinking.

Greek Christians became increasingly aware of the horrors awaiting the Greek Jews. When a trainload of Jews destined for Auschwitz stopped along the way, local villagers approached the train with curious trepidation.

> Some Greek Christians who encountered the train on one of its stops were horrified by what they saw, and spent hours going from car to car with water, bread, cheese and candles until the German guards intervened and sent them away.[135]

On August 7, 1943, the American Consul General in Istanbul, Burton Berry, wrote to Secretary of State Cordell Hull. Berry had interviewed a young Greek Jewish woman from Salonika who had escaped to Turkey after her husband, family and friends had been rounded up and sent to a concentration camp isolated from the city. Berry's detailed report included the following description of German actions:

> All Greek Jews were taken to the camp, whole families being carried off, regardless of age, sex or physical condition. Inmates of insane asylums and patients from hospitals, including incurable cases, and people suffering from infectious diseases were herded in with the others. All these unfortunate victims were confined for periods of varying length, while they were questioned regarding their property. In case the desired or expected information was not immediately forthcoming, the person questioned was subjected to various forms of torture. The German guards resorted to any expedient which they thought would produce confessions, but a favorite method of persuasion was the burning of finger tips, the procedure being repeated with increasing effectiveness upon each successive application. After this interval of examination, the Jews were sent off in cattle cars, almost without ventilation, 70

to a car. It was believed that their destination was Poland.[136]

Dr. Albert Menasse was a Jewish physician from Salonika who served as a medical officer in the Greek army. With his wife and sixteen-year-old daughter, he was deported to Auschwitz where he arrived on June 8, 1943. This is what he encountered when the door of the cattle car opened:

> German soldiers guard us while machine guns cover the area. The word *schnell* (fast) is heard continuously…In the general confusion, I do not see my wife and daughter. I am among a group of 300 men. After a painful march we enter the camp, which is surrounded by electrical fences. We see hundreds of emaciated people, dressed in rags, and working under brutal supervisors…We feel that a terrible drama must be unfolding in this place. I recognize someone else. He is Leon Yahiel, who was deported before us. He acts as an interpreter and says: "Prisoners, you are now in a death camp. Your wives and children, as I now speak to you, are

already dead. The buildings that you see in the distance are not factories. You are all alone. You have to work under terrible conditions, and each of you should try to do whatever he can to last as long as possible."[137]

The death rate on some cars was as high as fifty percent and the eyewitness reports filtered back to many Greek Jews yet to be deported. On June 20, 1944, the twenty-first Greek transport arrived at Auschwitz from Athens. Most of the 446 men and 131 women were from Corfu, and they had neither food nor water for twenty-seven days. Miklos Nyiszli was a Hungarian Jewish pathologist who was selected to serve as Dr. Mengele's coroner and as physician to the Sonderkommando. In his postwar memoir, he described what he saw:

> When they arrived at Auschwitz's unloading platform, the doors were unlocked, but no one got out and lined up for inspection. Half of them were already dead, and the other half in a coma. The entire convoy, without exception, was sent to number two crematorium.[138]

There were a number of Greek Jews living in Salonika who were Spanish citizens. The Germans separated them from the other Jews, but did not spare them from the same horrible fate. Jeanne Gattegno was one of those Spanish citizens:

All the Spanish citizens had been rounded up and taken to the synagogue, in order to be deported as well...We were shipped off to Bergen-Belsen by train. The trip was a nightmare in itself: we were put in cattle cars, packed like sardines in a can. There was hardly any food or water, and no room to sit. There was a bucket in place of a bathroom and no privacy, of course. It was horrible, and lasted for days, over an entire week. Many died before we ever reached the camp...Bergen-Belsen was a camp of slow death, death by starvation and disease. People died every day....When I got to Bergen-Belsen, I was seven months pregnant. I was having some trouble, and couldn't hold out any longer, so they took me to the hospital for an operation. The baby died there. How it died, I don't know...I was sent back to the camp. It was terrible, terrible, terrible...You can't describe it.[139]

The last transport left Salonika on August 10, 1943. The records of Auschwitz-Birkenau show that 48,974 Jews arrived there from Salonika. Of these, 37,386 were immediately gassed. [140] Having completed its work, the special German SS unit left Salonika and returned to Berlin.

On August 11, 1943, the Italian Consul General Castruccio, surveyed the empty streets of Salonika and wrote:

> The Jewish community of Salonika, which was founded before the discovery of America and which included around 60,000 members, exists no more...The liquidation of the Jewish community was carried out with the greatest atrocity, horrors, and crimes, such as never has been seen before in the history of all times and of all people.[141]

A young Greek Jew from Salonika, Vital Solomon Aelion, escaped from a German labor camp in the winter of 1942. He had heard reports of the transports from some of the Greek railway workers and decided that he was not going to be forced into a cattle car and sent to an unknown fate.

"I was 18 years old and I'd already seen enough. But from that point, I would experience a lot more."[142] Vital fled into the mountains and joined the resistance group ELAS. He was the first Jewish partisan in all of Greece and soon became a platoon commander. Thousands of Jews joined the resistance where they were christened "synagonistis" (comrades in arms), a title of honor among the resistance fighters.

Most of the Greek Christians in the resistance came from poor farm families and had little education. The Greek Jews, on the other hand, had an urban upbringing, were educated and often spoke several languages. Generally, they were held in high esteem, coexisted well with their Christian brothers- (and sisters) in-arms and shared a strong sense of solidarity against the enemy. Even before learning of the extermination camps, ELAS viewed the persecution of Jews as a heinous racial crime perpetrated against a defenseless people – a crime that affected all of Greece:

> We feel the pain of the downtrodden race just like ours. Every Greek should complain about the sufferings of the Jews

because it is a part of the suffering that the occupier has heaped on all the people who dwell on Greek soil. It is a part of the fascist brutality that strikes one or the other or all of us together.[143]

Jannina (Ioannina) in northwestern Greece, was one of the oldest Greek-speaking communities and one of the most highly acculturated Greek-Jewish communities in all of Greece. In fact, the Germans had some difficulty determining who was and was not Jewish.

The Germans didn't know on their own who we were, and how many of us there were…[So] the Germans took over the Jewish old folks' home. And they made an announcement that all Jannina residents from twelve and up had to come to the offices at the old folks' home, to get ID cards. As soon as you came in, on the right, in the Community Office, there were two police officers. As each person walked by, if they were Jewish, the police officer would [say] "Yuda," that's a Jew.[144]

News of the Salonika deportations had reached Jannina, but many of the Jews were convinced they had little to worry about. They were convinced by their inert, naive Rabbi, Shabtai Kabilli, who, like Rabbi Koretz of Salonika, urged them to stay in the city, obey the German orders and don't worry. They spoke Greek, enjoyed reasonably good relations with Greek Christians, and made substantial contributions to the local economy. It was reported that the SS commander in Jannina told the city's Jews that because they spoke Greek they would be treated differently – better – than other Jews in Greece.[145]

The quisling government collaborator, Prime Minister Ioannis Rallis, (who had replaced Constantine Logothetopoulos) reportedly made similar assurances to "the Jews of Old Greece":

We all know that they are loyal and have a conservative spirit, and therefore they are considered to be real Greek citizens. Therefore the Germans will never harass them.[146]

The deceit and hypocrisy were brazen. The Germans harassed, deported and killed Jews, and

Rallis, the collaborator and facilitator, made it easier for them. The Germans liked his administrative skills and called him a "courageous and hard fighter against communism." [147] Rallis organized a special police force (Security Battalions) of four thousand Greeks who were sent out to look for Jews and their Greek leftist protectors.[148] By the summer of 1944, there were over 16,000 members of these battalions. The Germans called the best of these units "Evzone Battalions" recalling the elite units of the Greek army.[149] Special assassination squads were formed and given lists of "communists" (basically anyone who opposed the Germans and their collaborators) from the Germans and the Security Battalions. These cold-blooded murderers operated in small groups, wore plain clothes and killed, wounded or kidnapped over 2,000 people.

Only about a hundred Jews escaped from Jannina. When the Germans began the roundup on March 24, 1944, 1,832 Janniote Jews, nearly the entire Jewish population, were collected in an hour, driven in trucks to a concentration camp at Larissa, and then put on a train to Auschwitz where they were murdered.

Chrysoula Politis was a survivor from Jannina. This is part of her remembrance of her deportation:

> On the trains, we were like animals in cars meant for horses...The windows were very small and covered with wooden planks so that we couldn't see outside. We began to sing and cry...Was it day or night? The sun rose and set, and we didn't know where we were going, what we were doing, where we were. We didn't know why we had been taken away. Nothing. We had nothing to eat; we had nothing. We were starving.[150]

Greek Jews had to travel much longer distances to reach Auschwitz-Birkenau. It took one to three days to reach Auschwitz from other points in Europe, whereas it took most transports seven to eight days from locations in Greece. It took twenty-four days to transport the Jews of Rhodes to Auschwitz. This greater length of time spent in cattle cars caused more suffering and more deaths.

> ...deprived of water and adequate food, cramped into suffocating quarters unable to lie down, forced to relieve themselves in

a bucket in the middle of the car, all
contributed to their debilitated state on
arrival...As reported by [an] eyewitness,
when the doors to the cattle cars opened,
there was dead silence.[151]

Those who survived deportation became
prisoners who were humiliated, tortured, starved
and forced to work at hard labor. Psychologist
Bruno Bettelheim, who spent a year in two German
concentration camps at Dachau and Buchenwald,
wrote of the Gestapo's desired results for operating
the concentration camps:

The results which the Gestapo tried to
obtain by means of the camps were varied.
Among them were: *to break the prisoners as
individuals* and to change them into docile
masses from which no individual or group
act of resistance could arise; *to spread terror
among the rest of the population* by using the
prisoners as hostages and by
demonstrating what happens to those who
oppose the Nazi rulers; *to provide the
Gestapo members with a training ground* in
which they were educated to lose all
human emotions; *to provide the Gestapo*

with an experimental laboratory in which to study the effective means for breaking civilian resistance, the minimum food requirements needed to keep prisoners able to perform hard labor when the threat of punishment takes the place of other incentives, and the influence on performance if the prisoners are separated from their families.[152]

The physical hardships and psychological trauma caused many deaths. Bettelheim described how he was able to survive:

The writer feels that he was able to endure the transportation and what followed, because he convinced himself that these horrible and degrading experiences somehow did not happen to "him" as a subject, but only to "him" as an object. The importance of this attitude was corroborated by statements of other prisoners. They couched their feelings usually in such terms as, "The main problem is to remain alive and unchanged." What should remain unchanged was individually different and roughly covered the person's general attitudes and values.[153]

Many of the Jews of Zakynthos, like those in Salonika and Jannina, were unaware of the camps or of Nazi intentions and did not feel immediately threatened. The Jews of the island saw the strength and courage their Christian neighbors derived from their beloved Bishop Chrysostomos, and perhaps these acculturated Jews felt a vicarious security from that, or at least felt a reassuring comfort in knowing that this good and decent holy man cared about them as well as the Christians. But they were still fearful. The bishop's brother-in-law, Dionysios Stravolemos, wrote that when informed of Nazi atrocities,

> ...they trembled on hearing of it...but did not see it as immediately threatening them. They lived with a fear and were supported by hope. The fear was known. The hope was unknown. With that unknown, they marched on, continuing with their work...Things were unstable, unsteady and dangerous.[154]

The Jews of the island also heard stories of Greek thugs in other parts of Greece who were on the Gestapo payroll. These traitors would identify Jewish families in hiding and then blackmail them for money and other valuables in exchange for promising not to reveal their hiding place to the Germans. Once the collaborators got the money and valuables, they would turn the family in to the Gestapo. But in many cases, the tactic backfired. Jewish families were told by their Christian neighbors to ask for twenty-four hours to get the money and valuables together. When the thugs would return the next day, they would be ambushed by guerilla fighters or the local police who had been notified by the neighbors. Twelve-year-old Raphael Moissis and his family were in hiding in a small village near Athens when two Greeks tried to blackmail the family. He recalled what happened when the thugs returned the next day:

> I return now not to a story that I have heard from others but to a personal picture that I will never forget for as long as I live. I went out to the garden late that

night, with the tension of the ordeal that I had gone through, and with great surprise, saw that the bushes were moving even though there was not even a breeze. When I approached, I heard this voice coming out of the bush: "Go away, little fellow!" The Resistance had come down and surrounded our house, armed to the teeth and ready to give a battle, if need be to save our family.[155]

When the thugs returned the next morning, Raphael peeked through the window to watch the guerillas pounce on the Gestapo lackeys and take them away. Justice for these traitors was swift and sure. Seconds after they were apprehended, Raphael heard a series of gunshots.

CHAPTER 5

ATROCITIES

"Two or three junior officers went slowly
through the village and gave the dying mercy shots."

A 19-year-old German soldier
after the massacre of Komeno

The Red Cross had been working with a
number of Christian organizations to free
Chrysostomos from prison in Athens. The
Germans figured it would be a smart move to free
the bishop, who could be helpful in identifying the
Jews on the island. They permitted the flying of the
Greek flag on government buildings and even
tolerated the singing of the Greek national anthem
during an emotional service in the Metropolitan
Church in memory of Greeks who died on the
Albanian front. The German military commander
attending the service announced that as a gesture
of good will, the bishop would be released from
prison. Eight days later, on November 23, 1943, the
bishop returned to Zakynthos. The only newspaper

of the island, *Action*, published clandestinely and circulated from house to house at night, wrote:

> After ten months of persecution by the Italian despots, the bishop has returned to us. The joyful pealing of the church bells greeted his arrival. He expressed his joy at seeing Zakynthos again and called for the people to unite for the good of Greece…Our tender father, the merciful one, the most compassionate, was once again with us. Zakynthos loved him so much.[156]

Immediately upon his release from prison, Chrysostomos saw what famine and war had done to the citizens of Athens. He saw emaciated figures gather each morning to look for scraps of food in the garbage behind the Grand Bretagne Hotel. He saw children aimlessly wandering the streets begging for food. He saw dead bodies on the sidewalks and streets. This is what historian Mark Mazower called "Germany's New Order:"

> In Greece, famine, inflation and expropriation had produced a profound sense of alienation from the Axis

cause...the New Order...The Germans had broken apart the existing structures of Greek society. They had failed to legitimize their presence or to create a new sense of solidarity in a common enterprise. It was to be left to the Greeks themselves to try and recreate the sense of community which would allow them in the first place to survive and, perhaps, to find a new sense of purpose in resistance, mutual assistance and planning for the future.[157]

Chrysostomos had plenty of time to think while in prison, specifically, to think about a strategy for dealing with the Germans. He had an ace up his sleeve, or more likely, under his *phelónion* (liturgical vestment). The ace was language – he spoke fluent German, which he learned during the years he spent at university in Munich. He would speak to and negotiate with the occupiers in their language. He would use language to create an understanding, an affinity, a compromise, anything that would help him keep his flock safe.

On the day of his return to the island and following the welcoming celebration, the bishop had two visitors, the German commander on the island, Alfredo Litt, and Paoul Berens, head of the German guards. They also brought an interpreter. The Germans introduced themselves, welcomed the bishop back to the island and stated their wish to have a friendly, cooperative relationship with him and the Greek people. There was no mention of the island's Jewish citizens. Chrysostomos could sense the profoundly immoral and malevolent natures of these two depraved criminals. The abstractions of evil and devil and hell had anthropomorphized before his eyes. His home, a small, modest whitewashed structure of stone, clay and mud was being invaded and desecrated by a killing force that knew nothing of love or pity.

When the bishop spoke, the Germans were stunned. They were thrilled to hear him speak fluent German (he also spoke French and Hebrew), and impressed to learn that he had lived and studied in Germany where he had actually met the Führer. Litt seemed genuinely pleased to encounter a worldly, educated man on this remote Ionian island. As the bishop's brother-in-law recalled, "On hearing him speak their mother tongue and on learning that he had lived for years and studied in

Germany, they were so enthusiastic about him that they thought of him as one of their own."[158] The bishop however, did not think of them as one of *his* own. He proceeded with his strategy and played his hand, which worked astonishingly well. He had their attention and their respect, although there was something about Berens' cool, detached manner that was disconcerting. How sad and tragic, thought the bishop, that these two creatures had devolved from the cultured and sophisticated people he knew in Munich as a student.

Nikolas Sartopos was a poor farmer who got himself arrested for possession of dynamite, a crime which carried the death penalty. He was languishing in the Zakynthos prison awaiting trial when the bishop started a dialogue with the Germans to free him, and he succeeded. When a German wireless telephone was found hidden in a village, fifty Greeks were rounded up and brought into a public square to be shot. The bishop ran to Commander Litt and pleaded with him to spare these people. Litt was impressed with the bishop's impassioned entreaty, but told him that he had orders and had to perform his duty. The bishop offered his own life instead, and Litt finally backed down. Other islanders were arrested and accused of being communists. Time and again, the bishop came to their rescue. But as he was soon to learn, saving Greek Christians was much easier than saving Greek Jews.

Saving people from starvation was also becoming more difficult. The islanders had been getting food from the Swiss Red Cross and supplies from Sweden. But Allied aircraft bombing and attacks by British naval ships cut off the supply routes and the deliveries stopped, causing additional hardship and suffering.

The only medical supplies on the island were in the German hospital and it was virtually impossible for any of the Greeks to get access to medicine or health care. Four young Jewish girls who were suffering from some terrible skin condition went to the bishop's sister for help. Vasiliki Stravolemos, like her brother, was strong-willed, courageous and determined to help the people of her island any way she could. The girls were students at the Professional School, which had been created by the bishop before the war. Their hands, faces and bodies were covered with rough, red patches and oozing sores. They were suffering from itching and pain and begged Vasiliki to take them to the German hospital. The naïve girls didn't know the risks involved. Two of them did not have false Christian IDs or baptismal certificates. Vasiliki told them horrific stories of what Germans had done with young women in other Greek islands and cities. She explained that the Germans would know they were Jewish which could endanger them even more. Vasiliki recalled that the girls persisted: "With the life we are living, it would be better if they killed us, let us rest in peace."[159]

After consulting with the girls' families, Vasiliki agreed to take them to the German hospital, which was in the town of Akrotiri, located on the eastern coast of the island just a mile or two north of Zakynthos city. As they approached the hospital, two armed German guards stepped forward and blocked them from entering. In flawless German, Vasiliki told the guards she wanted to see the chief doctor. The guards, surprised to hear a Greek speaking German, explained that no one was permitted to enter the hospital grounds without authorization. Vasiliki insisted that the girls needed immediate medical attention and begged the guards to call someone. Several minutes later, another guard appeared and escorted them into the hospital where they met an officer who took them directly into the hospital administrator's office. Seated in a plush leather armchair behind a desk was the doctor, described by Vasiliki as "a handsome youth with piercing eyes." He offered his hand to her and directed them to sit down. He asked what she wanted.

> I will speak to you sincerely and it rests with you to consider it. These sick women are Jews and I am Greek. I am mentioning this, not to a German doctor, but to a doctor of people, who, as all doctors of the universal practice take the oath of the Greek father of medicine, Hippocrates, to treat all men, irregardless of color, race or origin. I hope and believe and beg you to look at them. They are in need of you. Please accept to help them.[160]

The doctor's face softened. He asked where and how she learned to speak German so well.

> I lived in Germany for five years, when the Führer had begun to enter into politics,

133

and I studied at the University of Economics, along with my brother, Metropolitan Bishop of Zakynthos, Chrysostomos, when he was studying philosophy and law.[161]

The doctor seemed genuinely enthused. Without saying a word, he pressed a button on his desk and shortly thereafter two nurses appeared in the office. They were instructed to treat the four girls for acute psoriasis. This was not the last time Vasiliki would bring patients to the German hospital.

◆　◆　◆

The Gestapo came to Zakynthos shortly after the bishop's release from prison. The arrests, beatings and imprisonments continued at an accelerated pace and when the bishop tried to intervene, the Gestapo refused to see him. This intrusion was ominous. The bishop and the guerillas heard reports from Italian radio which revealed that the Gestapo had been registering Jews in both the Italian and German held parts of Greece. The reports about a camp in an Athens suburb were particularly horrifying. Two months before the bishop's release from prison, the Germans established the largest and most notorious camp in all of Greece, the Haidari concentration camp, not far from the prison where Chrysostomos was held. The Gestapo interrogations at Haidari resulted in routine beatings, torture and deaths. Over 21,000 people passed through Haidari, including Jews, Italian prisoners of war and Greek political prisoners. The Jews were transported to Auschwitz while over 2,000 prisoners were killed at the camp, including 200 hostages who were randomly chosen for execution in a single day at a nearby firing range. Chrysostomos figured he wasn't sent to Haidari because the Germans on Zakynthos were hoping he would collaborate with them in rounding up the Jews of the island.

The atrocities and mass executions at Haidari were unusual in number compared to other camps and prisons in Greece, and that was by design. As one Greek writer explained:

Haidari was founded more for the benefit of those outside than the inmates…It was to become widely feared, synonymous with death, and thus to enter the imagination of our vulnerable people.[162]

After the war, a team of Greek psychologists noted that the purpose of the inordinate number of killings and brutalities at Haidari was not to inflict punishment for "crimes" nor to prevent further unlawful activities, but rather to establish a reputation as the quintessence of the Nazi terror system – a system designed "...to extinguish the will and the imagination of the subject population. Hence, the conditions in the camp and the behavior of the guards were designed to put the inmates in constant fear of their lives."[163]

The atrocities at Haidari were part of a strategic plan, but the burning of villages and the killing of innocent people were often random and mindless. These acts were unfathomable and disturbing to many German soldiers who were ordered to burn and kill. The village of Komeno was sixty miles directly north of Zakynthos. In August, 1943, a two-man German reconnaissance team drove into the village and believed they saw evidence of *andartes* presence. The German troops were suffering from the effects of the summer heat, mosquitoes, and mounting casualties from partisan sniper fire. Their commander, Colonel Josef Salminger, frustrated because of his unsuccessful anti-guerilla operations in northwestern Greece, was determined to wipe out a guerilla lair, somewhere, anywhere. Salminger was a young, much-decorated regimental commander with a fanatical allegiance to the Führer. He referred to his 98th Regiment as "a regiment for Hitler."

On the evening of August 15, 1943, Salminger ordered an attack on the village. Before dawn the next morning, one hundred men set off in lorries for Komeno. Their company commander, Lieutenant Röser, a former Hitler Youth leader, gathered his troops and gave the order to advance into the village and, as became etched in the minds of his men years later, "leave nothing standing."[164] In minutes, the village was encircled and two flares were fired, giving the signal to begin the attack. Armed with rifles, machine guns and grenades, the assault troops moved quickly. In the first minutes of the assault, the village priest came running, waving his arms in protest. Röser himself shot the priest at point blank range. The troops stormed the homes and shot people as they slept. Those who tried to escape were mowed down by machine gun fire from soldiers manning guard posts on the outskirts of the village. Men, women and children were killed. No one was spared. The entire village was burned to the ground, leaving a grim, nightmarish scene of bodies shot and burned to death in their beds, sitting in chairs or crawling on the ground.

Lieutenant Röser was proud of his work. Around noon, he rushed back to his camp with a report for his commander and an invitation to see the good work his men had done. Many of the soldiers themselves, however, were sickened and conflicted:

> After the shooting it was very quiet. Most of the comrades were very depressed. Almost none agreed with the action.[165]

A nineteen-year-old conscript recalled:

Everything was quiet. I went into the village with some other comrades. Bodies lay everywhere. Some were still not dead. They moved and groaned. Two or three junior officers went slowly through the village and gave the dying mercy shots. [166]

There had been no return fire, no German casualties and no guerillas in the village. In Athens, on the day after the attack, a young German intelligence officer, Lieutenant Kurt Waldheim, entered this information into his unit's War Diary:

In the area of 1st Mountain Division, the town of Komeno is taken against heavy enemy resistance. Enemy loses.[167]

Years later, a former soldier who took part in the attack recalled that

...the outcome wound me up so much that even today I am not free of the terrible memories...I have never talked about these executions with anyone, not even my wife, although the whole business continues to affect me.[168]

But unlike these German soldiers, the former intelligence officer, Lieutenant Kurt Waldheim, had no recollection of the massacre. The man who would become President of Austria and UN Secretary General lied about his wartime service, claiming that his military career ended in 1942 after he was wounded in a battle on the Russian front. Witnesses, photographs, medals, commendations and his own signature on documents such as his war diary entry on the Komeno massacre exposed his deception. As one historian told the *New York Times*: "The fact that Waldheim played a significant role in military units that unquestionably committed war crimes makes him at the very least morally complicit in those crimes."[169]

News of the massacre at Komeno reverberated throughout Greece. Today, in the center of the main square, a marble monument contains the engraved names of the 317 villagers who died during the attack. In terms of age, they range from one-year-old Alexandra Kristima to seventy-five-year-old Anastasia Kosa. They include seventy-four children under ten, and twenty entire families.[170]

It wasn't only the Germans who committed these attacks on villages and civilians. Colonel

George Poulos was a notorious collaborator who, with a Greek-speaking Wehrmacht sergeant named Fritz Schubert, committed many acts of treasonous brutality and murder against his own people. The Nazis were financing what became known as "death squads" whose mission was to counter the rise of ELAS by spreading terror across the countryside. Poulos and his men would go into a village, randomly beat and kill people, take the victims' clothes, shoes, money and valuables, and then burn their houses. German officers from the local garrison would stand by approvingly, often taking photographs.

A Swiss Red Cross worker travelling across the country issued this report on atrocities in the villages:

> ...in Verria...twelve women had been raped; in the village of Skylitsi...Poulo's men had shot whomever they met; and, most horrible of all, in the village of Hortiatis...dozens of villagers had been slaughtered.[171]

After the war, Colonel George Poulos was tried as a war criminal, found guilty, and executed.

Even before news of the massacres at Komeno, Haidari and elsewhere reached Athens, the Jews of the city went into hiding. Alfredos Cohen, an Athenian lawyer, had vivid memories of life during the occupation:

> I will never forget the terror which seized us one night while I was hiding my large family in one of the houses, when it was announced that the Germans had published an order declaring that all Jews who were caught in hiding would be shot, and the people who were hiding them would be sent to the concentration camp.

> Then one of us said that it was not right for us to stay in that house and endanger the lives and peace of aged people and even women. The answer was: "No, you must stay. Indeed my son, why should our lives be more precious than yours?" [172]

While the Germans had their Security Battalions, assassination squads, and brutal collaborators, the resistance had its own system of justice, unencumbered by due process. Clandestine publications listed Greeks who were collaborating with the Germans. They were tried in guerilla courts and sentenced to death. Their names were published and executions were carried out by EAM/ELAS assassination squads (OPLA). The assassins were recruited from youths between the ages of eighteen and twenty-two who operated in villages, towns and cities, shooting their victims at close range or tossing hand grenades. Quisling government officials were prime targets and according to German war records, five to ten persons were killed each day by these youthful assassins.[173] In the first six months of 1944, OPLA picked off some prime targets, including the quisling minister of labor, the prefect of Euboea and the sub-prefect of Patras, while kidnapping the prefects of Chalkidike, Cephalonia, Lamia and Macedonia. Guilt by marital association was considered a punishable offense, as wives of alleged collaborators were also condemned to death.[174]

Chrysostomos begged and pleaded with the *andartes* on Zakynthos to refrain from committing these kinds of atrocities. He was not always successful.

CHAPTER 6

THE ORDER

"I thought of the bishop. I told him the story.
The bishop answered,
'You will not give any list to the Germans.' "
Loukas Carrer, Mayor of Zakynthos

Loukas Georgios Carrer was a good and decent man, liked and trusted by both Christians and Jews of Zakynthos. He was their mayor. Carrer felt helpless as the Germans began selecting able-bodied men to build fortifications for their artillery base in Kalamaki, near the southern coast of the island. Jewish workers, when discovered by the Germans, would be humiliated, beaten and sometimes tortured. The mayor was shocked and sickened when he learned how the Germans were treating the workers. Carrer worked out a deal with the Germans whereby he would be responsible for providing the workers. He made sure no Jews were sent to Kalamaki.

Carrer, a quiet, sensitive man, was a good negotiator. When the Germans issued an order for all Jews to report every other day to the Jewish community president, the mayor explained that such an order was unworkable since most of the Jews on the island were itinerant merchants and artisans who travelled to distant cities and villages to sell their wares and offer their services. The Germans accepted this fabrication and the order was rescinded.

Carrer's widow, Lily, would reminisce years later about her husband and the bishop:

> They were really afraid, actually terrified. It was dangerous. They could be caught and jailed and possibly tortured by the Germans...but no Christian betrayed the Jews. It was the general spirit of the time. It wasn't just the bravery of the mayor and the bishop. No Zakynthian turned in any Jewish name, not one. They were actions of duty, my husband's and everyone else's toward our fellow man. We did not consider Jews different from ourselves.[175]

Carrer had only perfunctory dealings with the Germans until the fateful morning in December, 1943 when Paoul Berens, Head of the German Guards, summoned him to his office. The mayor was offered coffee but politely refused. Berens, a small man with thick glasses that exaggerated his eyes, ordered Carrer to prepare a list of every Jewish family on Zakynthos. Carrer knew of the massacre at Komeno several months earlier, and was aware of the deportations from Salonika and other parts of Greece. He dreaded the day, this day, that he would be asked to collaborate with these murderous occupiers. He explained that the order was unnecessary because the Jews of the island were peaceful citizens who had lived on Zakynthos for generations. Berens interrupted the mayor, demanding the list in seventy-two hours. Carrer continued his protestation, arguing that the Greek Jews were an integral part of society, contributed to the economy and were a threat to no one. The head guard, like his commander, Litt, was fond of using his weapon as a tool of emphasis and intimidation. When the mayor stated that the Jews of Zakynthos were his friends and neighbors, Berens had enough. He went into a rage, shouting and threatening the mayor. He pulled his gun from its holster, put it to the mayor's chest and told him for the last time that he expected a list of all the island's Jewish families within seventy-two hours. Carrer was shaken as he left the meeting. His first thought was to go see the bishop:

> I thought of the bishop. I knew the bishop of Zakynthos, Chrysostomos was brave and extremely patriotic. I went to find shelter with him. I told him the story with all the details. The bishop answered me with courage: "You will not give any list to the Germans. I will take care of it myself."[176]

Chrysostomos was surprised that the Germans had ordered the mayor to compile a list of Jews instead of going to the chief rabbi, as they had done in Athens and other cities. Many Jewish families who had fled persecution in Salonika and other parts of northern Greece had found a safe haven in Athens, where Archbishop Damaskinos and Athens Police Chief Angelos Evert (both honored as "Righteous Among the Nations") created several thousand false baptismal certificates and more than 27,000 false identity papers.

In September, 1943, one month before Chrysostomos' release from prison in Athens, the Germans began their efforts to identify the Jews in that city. The Germans had sent Dieter Wisliceny to Athens to round up the Jews. Wisliceny, a violent, treacherous man, was a deputy of Adolph Eichmann, the administrator of the Nazi final solution. Wisliceny ordered Chief Rabbi Elias Barzilai to provide information about the Jewish population of Athens and to create a *Judenrat* (Jewish council) that would coerce people to join and make them compliant and responsible for keeping law and order in the Jewish community. The *Judenrat* would serve as a liaison between the German authorities and the Jewish population. Barzilai would be the president and would create a Jewish police force to carry out Nazi orders. Barzilai was given three days to provide addresses and other information about the Jewish community. A friend of the rabbi recalled that Wisliceny assured Barzilai,

> If you follow all these instructions, we will make sure that you receive special treatment, as we did in Salonika for Dr. Koretz [the chief rabbi who, with his entire family, was deported to Auschwitz].[177]

The demands sickened the rabbi. He was being asked to collaborate with murderers who wanted to exterminate his people. Like Mayor Carrer, Rabbi Barzilai, shaken by this encounter, went immediately to see the highest ranking Orthodox prelate, Archbishop Damaskinos. Both men knew of the Salonika deportations, and intelligence they had received from the Red Cross in Geneva was alarming -- there was no trace of the Salonika deportees.

These two men of God were not naïve. They were under no illusions about the Nazi game plan. Within the next few days, Barzilai destroyed the Jewish community records and advised the Jewish citizens to hide or flee. The three-day deadline had passed and Barzilai knew he was a marked man. A plan was hatched by Kostas Vidalis of the resistance group EAM and on the fourth day after the German order was issued, the guerillas went into action. Early on a Sunday morning, a group of men went to the rabbi's home, hid him, his wife and daughter in a mail truck, and drove them into the hills of central Greece where they survived the war working with the resistance. The Germans were not pleased with this turn of events. They issued a decree ordering all Jews to register within five days or risk being shot. Out of an estimated 8,000 Jews in the city, only 1,200 registered.

News of Rabbi Barzilai's flight to the mountains spread quickly. Other rabbis were left with an unambiguous circumstance and two models of behavior: react to German imperatives with compliance and subservience (Koretz) or with escape and resistance (Barzilai). The rabbis of Zakynthos, Volos, Larissa and other places chose the Barzilai model.

Meanwhile, Damaskinos organized a cadre of Greek Orthodox priests, police and resistance members and ordered monasteries and convents to shelter Jews. Priests were urged to tell their congregations to hide Jews in their homes. More than 250 Jewish children were hidden by Orthodox clergy alone, but at a price – over 600 priests were arrested, killed or deported because of their actions in helping Jews.[178]

Damaskinos and his priests actively encouraged and quickly arranged mixed marriages with no thought of religious adherence or conversion. They urged labor union officials and national organization heads to protest to German authorities, and they worked with the resistance to coordinate illegal Jewish immigration from Greece to Turkey to Palestine via fishing boats that left every two weeks. Jewish families, especially children, were hidden in monasteries until boats were available to rescue them. There is a historic singularity to these events as noted by Holocaust historian Yitzchak Kerem:

> Greek Orthodox monasteries provided refuge for Jews waiting for boat connections to Turkey. Unlike the churches in Northern Europe, there are no instances where those in hiding in religious orders were converted to Christianity, and after the war, children were returned to their parents or the Jewish community.[179]

Greek Jewish refugees in Jerusalem brought news of the bishops and priests who gave them food, shelter and clothing. This prompted Benzien Ouziel, Chief Rabbi of the Holy Land, to write to the Greek Consul for Palestine and Trans-Jordan on July 10, 1944:

> These immigrants...express undoubted praise and admiration for the archbishop of Athens who did everything possible, physically and morally, in his instructions to and influence on all the Churches and clergymen to preach compassion and give assistance to their Jewish brothers, and in his protest and defence before the authorities with courage and strength that adds to him and his Nation hounour and praise...I therefore hereby express to you, in my name, in the name of all your subjects who escaped and are escaping death and in the name of the whole Jewish Nation my most sincere thanks to the whole Greek nation and its great spiritual leader for this brotherly help which will remain and be remembered forever in the annals of Israel and the world.[180]

Damaskinos was the model and inspiration for all the bishops and priests in Greece. He also inspired those around him, including his peculiar neighbor, Princess Alice of Greece and Denmark, who lived across the street from him in a modest flat in the center of the city. Princess Alice had been born in Windsor Castle and was a great-granddaughter of Queen Victoria. Damaskinos was fond of the Princess and warned her to be careful, since there were always German guards on duty in front of their residences.

At an early age, the Princess was diagnosed with congenital deafness, but could still speak, albeit with indistinct pronunciation. A precocious student, she learned to read and speak English, German, French and Greek.

Alice married Prince Andrew, son of King George I. When her husband served in the Greek army during the Balkan Wars, she too served, working as a field nurse, assisting at operations and setting up field hospitals. During the German occupation, while most of the royal family remained in exile in Egypt, Alice stayed in Athens, worked for the Red Cross, organized the largest soup kitchen in Athens, and traveled to Sweden to bring back medical supplies on the pretext that she was visiting her sister, wife of the Crown Prince.[181]

During the first year of the German occupation, mass starvation caused tremendous suffering and many deaths throughout Greece. In Athens alone, five hundred to a thousand people, mostly children, died every day. Alice herself suffered, losing twenty-six kilos in weight during the harsh winter of 1941.[182] In December, Prime Minister Emmanuel Tsouderos of the Greek government in exile in London wrote to President Roosevelt explaining that "the brutal Germans have long since discarded respect for any law and their only object is the reduction of the world by fire, sword and famine."[183]

Alice's soup kitchen served starving children dry bean or chickpea soup, cooked in large cauldrons over wood fires. When available, she would add some parsley, onions or olive oil, strictly measuring and monitoring all of the ingredients. After the children were fed and if there was a surplus, she opened the doors to the hungry parents waiting in the street outside.[184]

Alice also organized shelters for orphaned children (one for girls and one for boys) and a nursing circuit for poor neighborhoods, where she organized groups of nuns who visited and cared for the sick and destitute in their own homes. She was often seen walking the deserted streets after curfew distributing food and rations to children and policemen.[185]

Before the German occupation, the Princess enjoyed racing through the streets of Athens on her motorcycle, a cigarette clenched between her lips. After the occupation, she gave up the motorcycle and drove a car, delivering supplies throughout the city, including seventy-seven liters of petrol a month she got from the Swedish Relief Commission.

When Princess Alice heard of a Jewish widow, Rachel Cohen, and her five children who were in desperate need of refuge, she took them in. The Germans became suspicious and visited her on several occasions. She was even questioned by the Gestapo from time to time. On each occasion, she used her deafness as an excuse and pretended not to understand their questions until they left her alone. [186] Years later, one of Rachel's children, Alfred Cohen, wrote,

> She not only saved the lives of our mother, sister and Michel, but also the lives of all

the rest of us because we would never have dared to flee Greece while knowing the rest of the family were left behind totally unprotected.[187]

Princess Alice had five children of her own – four girls and one boy, Philip, the youngest of the children who years later became Prince Philip, Duke of Edinburgh, the husband of Queen Elizabeth. In film and photographs of the royal family, a small nun in black habit was often seen in the background, smoking a cigarette. That was Princess Alice, who became a Greek Orthodox nun after the war. During a ceremony at Yad Vashem honoring his mother with the title Righteous Among the Nations, Prince Philip remarked:

I suspect that it never occurred to her that her action was in any way special. She was a person with deep religious faith and she would have considered it to be a totally human action to fellow human beings in distress.[188]

There was no royalty on Zakynthos, no Princess Alice to help feed and hide people, no international connections with the Red Cross to facilitate the smuggling of supplies. Bishop Chrysostomos had closely followed the events in Athens and knew he had to act quickly. First, he needed to buy time. If he had to relocate and hide all 275 Jews of the island, he needed more than the three-day deadline given by the Germans. He would go see Head Guard Berens and pretend he knew nothing of the order to the mayor. In the course of the conversation, Berens revealed that he had ordered Carrer to compile a list of all the island's Jews, adding that they were to be arrested. This new information, the fact that they would be arrested, alarmed and infuriated the bishop. In his fluent German, he protested with righteous and passionate indignation:

> The Jews of Zakynthos are obedient subjects of Greece and are good, peace-loving, hard-working members of my flock. They are pureblooded citizens of Zakynthos. They are not dangerous. Please do not enact this measure in Zakynthos. It would be a great crime.[189]

As he waved his shepherd's crook in the air punctuating his outrage, the German responded with Luger histrionics, although the weapon did not intimidate the bishop. Berens, like a broken record, kept repeating that he had orders. The two men finally agreed that they would seek the intervention of Captain Alfredo Litt. This was a victory in the bishop's mind, since he felt a better rapport with Litt, a man he perceived as more civilized than the coarse Berens. The meeting was to be held the next day.

Litt seemed genuinely pleased to see the bishop, although the cordial air of their first meeting had become polluted as a result of the bishop's incessant interventions. Litt calmly explained that he had an order from the Axis high command and was obligated to fulfill it. This prompted a conversation about duty. The bishop, unimpressed with the captain's piffling pedantry on military duty, was reminded of another German's reflections on duty:

> What destroys a man more quickly than to work, think and feel without inner necessity, without any deep personal

desire, without pleasure—as a mere automation of "duty."[190]

Ironically, the same German philosopher and poet, Frederic Nietzsche, greatly influenced Hitler's worldview (will to power, death of God, master-slave mentality, herd instinct, ascendancy of a master race (*Herrenrasse*), a superman *(Übermensch)*, and existence of subhuman life forms *(Untermenschen)*.[191]

Litt, to the bishop, was not a man, but a machine, an articulate automaton with no soul, no conscience, nothing but a pathetic pawn in Hitler's ghastly scheme to annihilate an entire race.

The bishop was using a different approach with Litt than he had with Berens. He softened his tone and listened patiently. He asked questions, suggested alternatives and said he understood when told that Litt's own life would be in danger if the order were not obeyed. A fleeting storm of cognitive dissonance swept through the bishop's mind. Would it be moral/ethical to sacrifice one hate-filled, murderous Nazi to save 275 Jews?

Litt and Chrysostomos agreed to meet again in a few days. This gave the bishop and the mayor more time to meet, contact the rabbis, the priests, the *andartes* and to begin planning a strategy. Persecution of Jews on the island (and Christians who tried to help them) was intensifying which meant that more vigorous resistance efforts were needed immediately. The priests and local authorities set about to accelerate their efforts issuing fake baptismal certificates and IDs to Jewish citizens. Over the next several days, a great conversion ensued on the island. Without a drop of baptismal water or a word of holy incantation, nearly all the Jews of Zakynthos became Christians.

CHAPTER 7

MALVINA MESSINA

"In some of the villages, they didn't know what a Jew was."
Malvina Messina

At age twenty-eight, Malvina Messina became Varvara Stravridou. The local Greek Orthodox priest, Father Georgios, had personally delivered the Christian identification papers to Malvina and her family. If the Nazis had caught him doing this, he could have been shot or hung from an olive tree.

The whole thing seemed so perfunctory to Malvina. There were no instructions, no warnings, nothing but the handing out of papers without hardly a word spoken. "Varvara, Varvara," Malvina repeated to herself. Her new identity did little to ease her trepidation. The Germans were searching houses of both Christians and Jews. Greek Christians were being arrested, shot or had their houses burned to the ground because they were suspected of hiding Jews.

Malvina's father, Elias, walked the priest to the door. She couldn't hear their short conversation, but witnessed their embrace and felt the power of love and humanity on that transformative day. She would not see Father Georgios again until the war's end.

Elias Messina was in the textile business and had a store that did a good business. He kept his money in bags hidden in the basement and in the fruit storage. Soon after the German occupation, the store was ransacked.

The Germans had allocated small amounts of flour to Greek Christians, but Malvina's family was too frightened to go pick it up. If the Germans suspected someone in the queue was Jewish, they would give them flour and then follow them home. Malvina's parents decided they would give their Christian name to a neighbor who would get the flour for them, at great risk to the neighbor.

The Messina family did not wait for the bishop or anyone else to tell them to go into hiding. Their home was severely damaged in an allied bombing raid and they were forced to leave. They headed into the mountains.

We were like refugees in the mountains. We managed to stay alive because we moved from village to village, always hiding, mostly in basements and fruit storage. We felt like criminals escaped from prison. It was a very bad experience. We lived in constant fear.[192]

Allaying the fear somewhat was the fact that few Germans were seen in the mountains, primarily because of the steep, narrow roads to the isolated villages, and because of the guerilla forces that occupied the mountains. And it was heartening for the Messina family to encounter good people in the villages, people who knew they were Jews but were still willing to help them:

They were really good people. They knew we were Jewish but they helped us and never betrayed us. They let us stay with them and gave us food and clothing. They loved us very much and we loved them.[193]

CHAPTER 8

RAPHAEL CONSTANTINOS

"They knew we were Jews. They didn't say a word."
Raphael Constantinos

The year was 1922. The Greek Navy commander on Zakynthos barked orders to the newly drafted recruits. Yeshayahu Constantinos was fairly certain that he was the only Jew in this ragged group of draftees, and was apprehensive about the confrontation he was about to have with this stern-faced military man. "Sir, I am a Jew and I do not wish to work on the Sabbath." To his surprise, the commander acquiesced with simply a word or two, and that was it, no work on the Sabbath. The encounter had an impact on young Yeshayahu who fashioned his thoughts and feelings into a short parable of human understanding and respect that he imparted to all his six sons.

Raphael, the oldest of the boys, was quite fond of his elementary school principal, a Christian man named Rennis, who had always been kind and friendly towards him. This was a Christian school, as there were no Jewish schools on the island. Raphael excelled in math, geography and history, and had studied his own family lineage, learning that his roots went back several hundred years to Spain, and that his original family name was Al-Constantini.

At age fifteen, Raphael decided to become a blacksmith, a trade he learned from his grandfather. All the schools on Zakynthos had closed during the war, which started with the Italian occupation a month after Raphael's bar mitzvah. He was proud of his work – sturdy barrels for olive oil and expertly made and repaired pots, pans and cups. During the Italian occupation, he would walk as many as twenty-five kilometers a day to find work, often trading his skills for barley, wheat, flour or olive oil. His father, an itinerant fabric merchant, also bartered his goods for food, recruiting his sons to carry the goods from distant villages. His mother stayed home with the younger brothers and sewed winter blankets.

The Constantinos family was poor, but enterprising. Raphael and his brothers would carry buckets of fresh water to the Italian headquarters at the port and trade them for scraps of food leftover from the soldiers' lunches. That, and many other things, changed when the Germans took over.

> The Italians surrendered and the Germans came. People were scared. Once, after curfew, they shot at me. I jumped in a ditch of mud and water and hid there for the entire night.[194]

Chrysostomos tried to intervene and get the Germans to loosen the curfew restrictions, but was unsuccessful.

> When the bishop came back to Zakynthos and heard about the curfew, he spoke to the Germans and tried to help us. He loved the Jews a lot.[195]

The Jews of the Zakynthos ghetto were anxious and fearful. But the Constantinos family lived in constant terror because they lived next to the largest of two synagogues on the island, and they knew that if and when the Germans decided to harass the Jews, those living near the synagogue would be the first to suffer. Raphael was too busy helping take care of his five younger brothers to worry about the Germans. And when he did think about the brutal occupiers, he was too scared to cry, but felt reassured by his maternal grandfather Isaiah's wisdom and his parents' strength.

Raphael noticed several newly arrived large boats at the port. He learned that the Germans had ordered a number of these charter boats from Patras, a port city on the Greek mainland about a hundred kilometers from Zakynthos. This was not a good omen. The guerillas had created a strong presence in this part of Greece and the Germans were committing horrible atrocities in retribution for guerilla activities. The worst of these was the massacre of Kalavryta on December 13, 1943. All male residents aged fourteen and older were ordered to gather in a field outside the village. The Germans opened fire with machine guns, killing 696. Only thirteen survived. The Germans then burned down the entire town, including the Monastery of Agia Lavra, the birthplace of the Greek War of Independence. (As a historical footnote, no German commanders who committed these atrocities were ever brought to justice. These included Major Ebersberger who carried about the destruction of Kalavryta, and Hauptmann Dohnert who commanded the firing squad.)

The Constantinos family was also aware of the Salonika deportations and the atrocious treatment of Jews in other parts of Greece. Raphael recalled years later that there was only one explanation for the boats: "The Germans ordered the charter boats from Patras for the Jews of Zakynthos."[196]

CHAPTER 9

ERKANAS TSEZANA

"We, the Jews of Zakynthos, have never forgotten our heroes."
Erkanas Tsezana

At age eleven, Erkanas Tsezana was a very talented musician. His Jewish band was a favorite, especially at weddings and even at Greek Orthodox religious ceremonies. Bishop Chrysostomos was particularly fond of him and loved his violin playing. But the music died when the Germans came. Erkanas and his family didn't want exposure to the occupiers.

Erkanas had many Christian friends. Nikos, his best friend, would help him hunt for food. "We were inseparable. I never felt different from my Christian friends."[197] But as Erkanas was to learn from his father and uncle, he *was* different – he was a Jew, and the Germans didn't like Jews.

His father, like many Jews on the island, was a fabric merchant. After his store was ransacked by the Germans, the family had to learn a new way to survive.

> Everything had changed. We had to adapt to new conditions and that meant a new way of life. My father and uncle bought some cattle, sheep, cultivated some land and started growing corn, squash and potatoes. We stopped being the spoiled kids of the city and became village children. We had to produce off the land. That was the only way we could live and survive.[198]

The Tsezana family never hid from their neighbors the fact that they were Jewish and fearful that the Germans would try to find them. The family knew the son of a local pharmacist who had just returned from Germany where he was studying medicine. The shocking news he brought terrified the family. He spoke of Jews being killed in concentration camps and crematoria, of horrific medical experiments and other acts against nature and humanity. With sad, bitter irony, Erkanas recalled how it could be that his family knew about the German atrocities but the Allies did not.

> The major powers of the world didn't
> know there were crematoriums but we in
> the little island of Zakynthos were
> informed by a student. The allied
> countries said they didn't know. We, a
> small group of Jews on Zakynthos, knew
> what was going on.[199]

This information traumatized Erkanas. He knew the Germans were brutal, but the news of the nightmarish fate awaiting his family affected him for the rest of his life.

> We were psychologically shattered…As a
> child, this thing takes root, becomes
> imprinted in your soul…Even now as I am
> saying this, I am scared…And I still have
> this fear…If I see a German in my dreams,
> I go into shock.[200]

When one watches the video testimony Tsezana gave some fifty-four years after Zakynthos was liberated, the voice and face and demeanor of this survivor reveal that he is still haunted by the memories, still traumatized by nightmares.

Anticipating the Germans' next move, the Tsezana family decided to leave for the mountains.

Erkanas and his father took pieces of the tin roof and melted them into kitchen supplies. They started trading the family jewelry for food and supplies. Erkanas remembered his mother trading a gold ring for two chickens and bushel of flour.

They moved in with a peasant family, who "...knew we were Jews. They took us in and put on their best clean linens and white sheets." When gunfire was heard, the family moved higher into the mountains, changing homes several times. Years later, Erkanas could still remember the names of some of his hosts, such the Bafakis and Roumeliotis families, and the love and kindness they showed their guests.

The hardships of hiding in the mountain villages took its toll on the Tsezana family, especially on the father, an educated, cultured man who spoke five languages. They were living in an abandoned home when the father started drinking. Erkanas had just turned twelve and mustered enough courage to confront the man he loved, admired and depended on.

I asked him what he was doing. He said, "If you knew who I was and how I've ended up, you would never have asked me that question." So I tried to uplift my father, telling him life goes on and he must be strong. Fear made us wise even before we grew up.[201]

The Tsezana family members were close and relied on one another to survive and minimize the fear and panic as they ran to hide from one mountain village to another. Erkanas was to learn later that this trait of familial and social cohesion didn't help Jews survive. He painfully reflected that "We were a patriarchal family, and unfortunately, this is what killed the Jews. They didn't take different paths. When they were found, they were found in bunches, groups, masses. Wherever the grandfather goes, everyone goes – children, grandchildren, relatives, neighbors – like a flock of sheep."[202]

Steven Bowman, Professor of Judaic Studies at the University of Cincinnati, points out that the tendency toward patriarchy and intense family loyalty of Greek Jews caused the death of entire families and prevented many young Jews from escaping into the mountains where they could fight or survive with the resistance.

[This] was perhaps the major factor in the loss of many young men and women. After arrival in Poland, for those men selected for destruction through work, a day or two often passed before they learned that their wives and children, mothers and fathers, grandparents and extended families were gassed and burned on arrival.[203]

To assuage the anxiety of a life in hiding, Erkanas created his own fantasy family.

When we went into hiding, I took some of my favorites things – some clown dolls, like theater marionettes. I made them into a mother, father, grandfather, kids, aunt and uncle. And I still have them.[204]

CHAPTER 10

ESTER DANTE

"I was the littlest guerilla."

Ester Dante

The bombings terrified ten-year-old Ester:

It was endless bombing. The shattered
glass from a bomb killed my grandmother.
Then one day, I remember Shlomo [Ester's
younger brother] was peeling oranges and
my sister and I were sitting on the floor
leaning against a wall. Then the house
started shaking. Suddenly it was dark,
then a siren. The wall we were leaning
against collapsed. It killed everyone in the
family who lived on the other side.[205]

The Dante family was large – her mother,
Sultana, father, Moishe, four brothers and sisters,
and two grandparents. The family was poor but
Moishe was a skilled tinsmith who often bartered
his services for food. "The Christians knew we

175

were a big family and would give him olives, beans, fruit and vegetables for his work."[206]

Even before the occupation, there was a true feeling of community and caring on the island. On Shabbat, the wealthier Jewish families would bring food to feed the less wealthy, and the "goy of Shabbat" (the Christians) would open their homes to the Jews so they could bring their uncooked foods and use Christian family ovens because of Sabbath restrictions.

The Dante family was good friends with their Christian neighbors and Ester recalled fond memories of their interaction:

> There were two large eucalyptus trees and some benches near our house, and every evening, the Greek men would gather there and would call dad to join them and they'd share cheese, bread and wine. If they saw me, they would invite me too. Later, when we didn't have any food, they would bring us bread and olives, whatever they had to share. We always knew we were Jews and as much as they were good to us, we always had the fear that someday, something would happen

to us, but nothing ever happened to us. The neighbors loved us.[207]

Ester also had fond memories of the three years her family spent living in Corfu, where her father went to find work. There was a large Jewish population (about 2,000) on the island and Ester had many friends. When her grandfather, who had remained in Zakynthos, got sick, the family returned. Looking back years later, Ester realized that "…if we had stayed a few more months in Corfu, we would have become soap." When the Germans occupied Corfu, they brutalized the Jews, looted their homes, put them on barges to the mainland where waiting trucks took them to Athens, then trains to Auschwitz. Unlike the heroic mayor of Zakynthos, Loukas Carrer, the German-appointed collaborationist Mayor Kollas of Corfu proudly proclaimed to the island's municipal council: "Our great friends, the Germans, cleaned our island of the Jews."[208] Over ninety percent of the Jews on Corfu were murdered. Armando Aaron, a Greek Jewish survivor on Corfu, remembered the tragedy:

Once the Germans occupied Corfu, they terrorized the population into submission. Demobilized Italian soldiers warned many Jews to hide in the mountains but nobody followed their advice...Among the 2,000 members of our community, there were no more than fifty to sixty people who escaped arrest.[209]

Chaim Constantinidis, the same age as Ester, lived nearby. His family heard of the atrocities on Corfu and was shocked and incredulous:

We didn't want to believe it. We couldn't believe that people could inflict such suffering on other people. We had never harmed anyone. Why would they hurt us? When they took the last Jews from Corfu we realized that our time was coming. But even then we were so close and attached to the Christians that we were waiting for them to tell us what to do, to protect us.[210]

For Ester, life on Zakynthos was not unlike life on Corfu. To her, the Italians on both islands did not seem oppressive. The soldiers stationed at a barracks near her home often gave her father work making and repairing pots, pans, buckets and washbasins. In return, he was given spaghetti and bread.

> The Italians, at first, were nice and polite. They planted flowers, played with the children, gave us food and sandals. They never asked if we were Jewish.[211]

The flowers soon wilted, the children were ordered to attend indoctrination camps and there were no more handouts, no more food or sandals.

> The Italian fascists came. They were mean. They beat up people. There was a lot of fear, both among Jews and Gentiles. The fascists were like a different kind of people. They would get drunk and start fights and beat people up.[212]

Ester was playing on the beach when the Germans first landed on the island, replacing the Italians. All the main streets of the town were occupied and machine guns stationed on both ends. A curfew was enacted, yellow stars were ordered placed on Jewish homes and a new wave of brutalities swept the island, even more horrific than those of the Italian fascists.

The Germans arrested two men who were putting up protest posters near the local theater and later that day, Ester saw a gruesome sight -- the bodies of the men hanging from poles with warning notes pinned to their shirts. She witnessed two men get apprehended for singing patriotic songs and then drowned in barrels of lime. She recognized one of the men as the nephew of the Christian family that would soon give her family refuge. And closer to home, a group of drunk and sadistic German soldiers forced her father and brother at gunpoint to walk through a minefield. She remembered her father telling her brother to walk behind him because "I don't want to see you die in front of me."[213] They survived the harrowing ordeal. Ester saw these and other crimes against humanity that became seared into her memory. The witnessing of these atrocities had a strange impact on the young girl. It made her less fearful and more resolved to help in the fight against the oppressors.

Ester once found herself in the middle of a gun battle between some resistance fighters who had ambushed a group of drunken German soldiers.

When the firefight broke out, the partisans grabbed me and hid me. I noticed one of the German soldiers was shot full of bullet holes and was still walking. The partisans saved my life and then walked me home. They were dressed like farmers and were carrying hand grenades in their baskets.[214]

We had a lot of contact with the partisans. They were hiding in the olive groves. We listened to them. They told us what to do...I would sit on a bench by the side of the road with baskets and count the number of Germans who came by. I counted the number of trucks and soldiers and then gave the information to the partisans...Sometimes they would give me a letter to take to someone in town. I made trips all the time to deliver messages. I wasn't scared at all.[215]

Ester Dante, at age ten, became the "littlest guerilla" on Zakynthos.

CHAPTER 11

THE BISHOP'S LIST

"Here are your Jews."

Bishop Chrysostomos of Zakynthos

Zakynthos is situated just west of a major tectonic fault where the European and Aegean plates meet, resulting in a history of earthquakes on the Ionian islands. In August, 1953, residents of Zakynthos noticed some strange things happening, like the rising and falling of water levels in their wells. Fearing a possible earthquake, many left their homes and camped out in the olive groves. Their fears were not unfounded. A series of four severe earthquakes struck the Ionian islands, killing and injuring thousands and causing widespread devastation. The third and most destructive quake, followed by massive fires, occurred on the morning of August 12, measured 7.3 on the Richter Scale and was felt throughout Greece.

The apocalypse on Zakynthos was worse than anything seen during the war. The island suffered the total destruction of its infrastructure. Only three buildings were left standing – the St. Dionysios Cathedral, the Church of St. Nicholas and the National Bank building. The edificial survival of only God and money was not lost on future poets, writers and cynics.

The first foreign ship to arrive with aid to the victims was from Israel. It carried equipment, medical supplies and pharmaceuticals. Shortly after the ship docked in the harbor, its captain read a declaration to the island's military doctor, Anastasios Marino: "The Jews of Zakynthos have never forgotten their mayor or their beloved bishop and what they did for us."[216]

Nearly all the island's archives housed in libraries, government offices, churches and synagogues were destroyed, mostly by the subsequent fires. Personal diaries, journals, memoirs, letters and other documents relating to the war were also lost. What remained were the memories of the people who survived. Fortunately for history and humanity, one important diary and one intact memory were saved – those of Dionysios

Stravolemos, the bishop's brother-in-law. His diary began on May 1, 1941, the day the Italians first occupied the island, and ended on March 26, 1945, the day the Nazis left the island.

Stravolemos wrote in his diary that when the bishop returned from his meeting with Head Guard Berens, the bishop told those around him, "If the mayor and I fail, I will follow the Jews and I will fall with them into the sacrificial furnace."[217]

The *andartes* were alerted as to the acuteness of the situation. The guerillas on the island pledged their support and prepared to assist in the evacuation and hiding of the Jewish citizens, or to fight to liberate the Jews if they were arrested. The resistance, however, was not unified. The leftist EAM was the largest of the resistance organizations and had earned the enmity of EDES (National Republican Greek League), the largest of the non-communist resistance groups. Toward the end of the war, these groups would begin a series of civil conflicts that would lead to the Greek Civil War. Both groups had been monitoring the situation on Zakynthos and according to the bishop's brother-in-law, leaders of the two groups made an unexpected pact:

These organizations monitored the bishop's desperate struggle and made the joint decision and agreed that if the attempts to save the Jews did not succeed, EAM and EDES of Zakynthos would join their two organizations on a patriotic basis, to battle the Germans in order to liberate the Jews from their hands and to protect them, no matter what the sacrifice.[218]

The 72-hour deadline was approaching. The bishop, the mayor, the priests and the leader of the Jewish community, Moses Ganis had warned every Jewish family on the island of the deadly dangers facing them. They were told to make immediate preparations to go into hiding. Samolino Fortes and his family were among them:

The bishop ordered us to leave to go to the villages, to disappear from the town, to shut our houses, taking whatever we needed and go to the villages. Not all together, one here, one there, one elsewhere and we left. The whole family left. We were seventeen people. We went to a place called Yuleyka and found people, the Rapsomaniki family. I'm still crying for them, so much love I have for them. It's them who saved us. Till today, every year, I visit them and I hug them. I kiss them and they kiss me.[219]

A child, Moses, was born into the Fortes family while they were in hiding. Shortly after his birth, the resistance sent word to the local priest, Father Kouremenos, that the Germans were heading toward the village. The priest warned the family and urged them to leave as soon as possible. Baby Moses was left with Katina Rapsomaniki and the family quickly departed to hide in another village. Katina took care of the infant for many months, until it was safe for the family to return. After the war, the family left for Israel. In 1976, Moses Fortes returned to Zakynthos. This is how he described his visit:

I am the child who was born during the occupation in 1943. My parents left me with their friends. I was three when I left and over thirty when I returned. I asked where the Rapsomaniki family lived. I entered and said, "It's me, little Moses."

As soon as the lady saw me, she started shaking and shouting, "My son has arrived, my son is here. My son has come from Israel. Come see my big boy!" We wept and she held me in her arms for a whole hour. [220]

Katina Rapsomaniki, a Greek Orthodox, felt very close to the Fortes family. "We were better than brothers and sisters. We were one family. We always remember those times and most of all, we respected their love for their religion. They are more religious than us."[221]

The narrator of a documentary film about Zakynthos, *The Song of Life*, summarized her impression of this emotional reunion:

This moment encompassed the entire meaning of my trip and expressed the true meaning of the word humanity. Mrs. Rapsomaniki was one of the many heroes of Zakynthos. She offered the gift of life to Samolino and his family and by doing so, breathed life into the generations to come.[222]

The Constantinidis family had a similar experience. Chaim was eleven-years-old when life on Zakynthos became fraught with danger:

> They [the Sakis family] gave us a room. There were seven of us, as well as a cousin of my father's along with his wife and child. The ten of us spent five months cooped up in there. We could see the Germans passing the house through the shutter slats. I will never forget those people who risked their lives to save us. In 1971, I went to visit unannounced. I knocked on the door. Sofia Saki opened...when she realized who I was she started sobbing. She wouldn't let me out of her arms.[223]

Unlike the ill-fated Jews of Salonika, Jannina and other cities and islands, the Jews of Zakynthos, like the Fortes and Constantinidis families, were told the truth and given a plan for survival. Their leaders understood the German intent. Their Christian friends and neighbors were ready to help. And the bishop, who was fond of telling his flock, "Be a good Christian, save a Jew," was willing to risk his own life to save them.

Chrysostomos worried that the Germans, like the Italians, would tire of his constant interventions and protestations and would have him arrested. He felt he could deal with Commander Litt, but the Gestapo was another story. Its past refusal to talk with him meant that they saw no usefulness in him. He could speak with Litt in the commander's native German, but could not trust the man. Litt was, after all, a Nazi – a man who took orders and obeyed them, a man who felt superior to an entire race of people, a man who could kill innocent people without hesitation or remorse. The dark angel allegories were no longer confined to pages of scripture. They were here on Zakynthos, incarnate with polished boots, symbols of hate and weapons of murder.

The bishop's brother-in-law recalled the tension and pressure as the deadline approached:

The bishop and the mayor could not relax, not even for a moment. They found themselves under the influence of a tense nervousness which terrorized them. Everyone lived with nightmares…these dramatic days tortured the bishop. He was continuously thinking about it. He formulated plans and made decisions. Finally, one afternoon, a thought came to light: to take refuge in Hitler. We decided to keep it secret. This decision would be the last shot.[224]

At the meeting, Alfredo Litt demonstrated an exaggerated reverence toward the bishop, and he greeted the mayor with a stilted, formal courtesy. Two guards were positioned on either side of Litt's desk and a smug, stern-faced Berens stood in the back of room, arms folded. His threats had failed to produce a list of the Jews, but now, here in the commander's office, he would relish watching the cleric and the politician squirm and obey orders. Priests, bishops, mayors and many others were being arrested, imprisoned or shot for protecting Jews on other islands. Everyone in the room knew it, and everyone knew that these were the consequences of not obeying orders.

The bishop took a step toward Litt. The two men were scarcely a foot apart as the bishop took a piece of paper from his pocket and handed it to the commander. In a quiet German undertone, the bishop uttered four words that would reverberate throughout the history of the Greek Holocaust:

"Here are your Jews."

Written in German and Greek were two names: "Chrysostomos of Zakynthos" and "Loukas Carrer, Mayor of Zakynthos." There was nothing else on the paper. The anger and outrage on the commander's face had a curious effect on the bishop. It displaced his fear with fury:

> According to your orders, you can arrest me and not them, and if that does not satisfy you, then I will show you how close I am to these innocent Jewish families. I will follow them in their dramatic march and along with them I will enter the gas chambers and the crematories.[225]

Berens, meanwhile, was going through emotional havoc. As head of the German guards, he was not accustomed to orders being disobeyed. The impudent defiance of this island cleric was more than the short, bespectacled Nazi could bear. He drew his 9mm Luger and took several swift steps toward Chrysostomos. But violence, at least at this particular moment, was not part of Litt's strategy. Without moving his icy, fixed gaze from the bishop, the commander extended his arm, stopping Berens. Mayor Carrer, standing a few steps behind the bishop, was frozen with fear.

Dionysios Stravolemos recounted this tense, historic moment and how Litt's demeanor changed, whether in reality or as a ruse:

> The Administrator [Commander Litt] was dumbfounded by the bishop's commanding, imposing and determined tone. He looked at him speechless. Never had he confronted such an offer...Its influence on Alfredo Litt's moral resources was tremendous. The relentless and hard soldier, the German officer who was all-powerful at that moment, submitted to the human being. The Administrator became pale and assured the bishop that he understood the attempt "to make an exception for the Jews of Zakynthos."[226]

Litt said he would take the issue to the Nazi High Command. It was agreed that the men would meet again. There were no handshakes or departing courtesies.

CHAPTER 12

THE BISHOP'S LETTER

"Dear Führer…Please do not arrest the Jews of Zakynthos."
Bishop Chrysostomos of Zakynthos

Ester Dante wondered why Father Giorgios, a Greek Orthodox priest, was coming to the synagogue.

There was a priest who always came to the synagogue and would pray. The kids asked what he was doing. He came to study the Torah, and to warn us about the Germans.[227]

The inquiring mind of the Orthodox priest led him to a better understanding of the faith of his Jewish friends and neighbors. The history of his own ancient faith and his knowledge of Greek philosophy were helpful in finding truth, meaning and wisdom in the Jewish faith. He came to understand the historic, social and intellectual relations between ancient Jewish communities and Hellenism and that Greek philosophy had an influence on how Jews began to philosophize about their own faith.[228]

Father Giorgios, a young, earnest man of God, was in awe of his friend and mentor, Bishop Chrysostomos, whose command to "save the Jews" was tantamount to a divine reason for being. The priest wanted to better understand and feel closer to these innocent, persecuted people and their faith. Like them, and like most Zakynthians, he was fearful of the Germans. But the fear motivated him to work furiously, creating false Christian baptismal certificates and IDs. And how thankful he was that the Orthodox church had the wisdom and compassion to allow married men to become priests. His young wife, Presbytera Katina, was his trusted helpmate and co-conspirator in the "conversion" of as many Jews as possible. Katina prepared the documents and made up Christian names while Father Giorgios signed (sometimes a dead priest's name) and delivered the documents.

The priest and his wife knew the risks they were taking. They heard stories of priests and bishops in Athens and other places that were arrested or shot for doing exactly what they were doing. They took comfort and strength from scripture:

> For you have been a stronghold to the needy in distress, a shelter from the storm and a shade from the heat; for the breath of the ruthless is like a storm against a wall. (Isaiah 25:4)

The allegorical "breath of the ruthless" was a very real and deadly storm brewing against the walls of every Jewish home on Zakynthos, but not every Jewish family was heeding the storm warnings. One family told the priest they wanted to stay in their home; their *yiayia* (grandmother) was too frail to move. The next morning, a cart with straw bedding and a donkey were brought to transport the grandmother to a mountain village.

When confronted with intransigence about moving, the priest ran to his bishop. A visit by the respected Chrysostomos usually did the trick. His bearing, his gravitas, his pleading were hard to resist. Before his next visit with the Germans, the bishop wanted to be sure that all the Jewish families were in hiding or making final preparations to leave for the mountain villages.

Days passed and there was no word from the Germans. The bishop and mayor did not trust Litt. They didn't trust that he passed along their entreaty to the German High Command. And even if he did, what were the chances that orders to arrest Jews would be stayed? Their paranoia was palpable. The days of waiting, hoping, praying were described as "...agonizing...desperate...the hardest and most nightmarish moments of their lives."[229]   Most accounts of what happened next have been obscured by the passage of time, fading memories and a sad dearth of historical records (lost in the earthquakes and fires of 1953). Thankfully, the bishop's brother-in-law recorded the event in his diary:

> He went to the Administrator...He had written an emotional appeal in German and handed it to the Administrator, with an entreaty to send it, by the German Administrator's wireless radio, personally to Hitler. He reminded Hitler that once, in 1924, when he was rushing forward in the first stages of his rise in politics, they had

met in Germany and they had exchanged thoughts about his national socialistic movement, and he begged him, "Please do not arrest the Jews of Zakynthos" personally guaranteeing along with the mayor that they were not dangerous, but "admirable and peace-loving."[230]

Everyone around the bishop shared his noble objective in protecting the Jews of Zakynthos, but not everyone agreed with his strategy and tactics. Presenting the "list" of Jews was defiant, risky, insulting and possibly counterproductive. The next maneuver, sending a letter to Hitler, could infuriate the man and incite him to take immediate action against what he would consider an obscure, obstinate island cleric who defied orders. A confrontational strategy that antagonized the Germans was a calculated risk that could result in the arrest or harassment of Jewish citizens, or reprisals against the entire population -- reprisals and retaliations that were already happening all over the island. These atrocities were swift and deadly: "Several witnesses saw the partisans capture a German guard and shoot him. The Germans leveled an entire village in retaliation."[231]

Chrysostomos listened patiently to the concerns of those who doubted him, but he knew that inaction was not an option. Archbishop Damaskinos in Athens and the resistance fighters on Zakynthos communicated harrowing accounts of what was happening all over Greece. Inaction and complicity meant certain death.

Several days after their meeting with the Germans, the bishop and the mayor were shocked to hear the early morning announcement on the loudspeaker. All Jews were ordered to leave their doors open, pack their suitcases and come to city hall to register. Clearly, Litt was trying to undermine the bishop, who was angered, but not surprised, by this duplicity and lack of good faith.

The bishop's strategy had a preemptive component that demanded noncompliance of German orders, unless those orders were issued at gunpoint. The strategy worked. The Jews who were packing suitcases were heading toward the mountains, not toward city hall. Not a single Jewish person on Zakynthos registered with the Germans.

The frustrated Germans went to "plan B." They started searching houses near the coast looking for Jews and for Christians who were hiding them. "They were searching houses for both Christians and Jews," recalled Malvina Messina. "We left when we saw them scouring the coastal suburbs…We saw them raiding and burning shops."[232]

For young Erkanas Tsezana, the flight out of the city was "…traumatic and dramatic. We had to leave for the villages. We left everything. We never went to school again. We always felt a sense of insecurity, so wherever we went, we made sure we had some things of value. My father gave us little bags of jewelry we could use in times of great need."[233]

The Constantinos family did not have bags of jewelry. Raphael, his parents and five brothers had little money when they left for the villages. "Almost immediately, all the Jews left the city for the villages. We found a room, 4m x 7m for two families. We split the room with a blanket."[234]

To impede Jewish flight out of the city, the Germans placed land mines on the roads leading out of town. Hertsel Matsa was a witness: "The roads were land mined. Only the fishermen knew what side streets were safe. We saw boats that we knew were brought to take us to concentration camps. They were coming to kill us."[235]

The Germans also tried sending platoons into the mountains to confront the *andartes* and look for Jews. That did not go well for them, as their officers had received no training on the actions of guerilla warfare. Many of the mountain roads were narrow, rocky and treacherous. The arid interior terrain was pathless, and the burning heat, harsh and tormenting. The Germans had few maps, a shortage of interpreters, and never enough drinking water. General Hubert Lanz, who commanded troops fighting *andartes* in other parts of Greece, complained of the guerillas' night attacks, bombing roads and bridges, blocking tunnels and mining open stretches of roadway. He tried flushing out the resistance fighters in the mountains, but this foreign, foreboding and unstable battlefield was problematic:

> Unfortunately, the terrain was altogether too inviting for guerilla warfare. High mountain ranges followed the road on both sides. On the long, partially wooded slopes were villages and many isolated

farm buildings. The partisans and those who assisted them lurked everywhere.[236]

Chrysostomos and Mayor Carrer were fearful that retreating German troops would destroy mountain villages on the way back to their base camp, especially if they had lost men on their unsuccessful excursions. Disproportionate retaliation was a common tactic. The Germans used flamethrowers, incendiary grenades or sometimes just petrol. They were methodical and efficient in the destruction of entire villages. In Agios Georgios, a small village in the mountains of central Greece, every house was burned to the ground, the wells were polluted with dead mules and all the trees and crops were destroyed. By July, 1944, according to a report of the Greek government in exile, 879 villages had been totally destroyed and 460 partially destroyed. [237] A shocking report from the Red Cross estimated that forty percent of the rural population "had their homes burned or looted and are in immediate danger of extinction."[238]

Chrysostomos beseeched his God for divine intervention. A simple volition of the Almighty

would solve the problem and save the Jews. The
bishop needed a miracle.

> And Moses stretched out his hand over
> the sea; and the Lord caused the sea to go
> back by a strong east wind all that night,
> and made the sea dry land, and the waters
> were divided.   (Exodus 14:21)

The exodus on Zakynthos would be less
dramatic, requiring less elaborate physical
phenomena, but a miracle nonetheless. Relocating
275 people from their homes to the mountains in a
matter of days was a small miracle in itself. Asking
God to convince the devil (Hitler) to spare the Jews
required grander supernatural complexities.

Chrysostomos believed that God was working
through him, that free will and good deeds could
save lives, but time was running out. He needed to
think and act quickly. He trusted God to give him
the courage, the wisdom and the stamina to save
his people.

> I will say of the Lord, "He is my refuge
> and my fortress, my God, in whom I
> trust." Surely he will save you from the

> fowler's snare and from the deadly
> pestilence. He will cover you with his
> feathers, and under his wings you will
> find refuge, his faithfulness will be
> your shield and rampart. You will not
> fear the terror of night, nor the arrow
> that flies by day...no harm will
> overtake you. (Psalm 91)

The bishop and the mayor knew that whatever response they received from Hitler, the Germans could not be trusted. They were ruthless murderers, fanatical in their zeal to kill Jews. Hitler's order, or lack of it, would have no effect on the evacuation strategy. All Jews in Zakynthos were in danger and were encouraged to leave as soon as possible for the mountain villages.

The Germans were facing another challenge which they referred to as the "second enemy" – mosquitoes. Malaria was causing many casualties, immobilizing more men than the *andartes* did. In the town of Elassona, eighty percent of a German company came down with malaria at least once. Camp beds and windows were draped with netting as German field doctors worked frantically to try to control the disease, while in Dachau, prisoners were being injected with malarial strains in order to find an effective vaccine.[239]

The Germans were contracting malaria at far greater proportions that the Greeks, which may have been attributable to the incidence of a genetic blood condition, thalassemia beta, prevalent in Mediterranean countries. The bishop and the mayor were not aware of this red blood cell phenomenon that may have protected them from contracting malaria, but were thankful for the timely infestation of the tiny blood-hungry creatures who were distracting and discomforting the enemy. The bishop was grateful for all the help he could get, and from whatever source it came.

> I will smite them with pestilence and
> dispossess them, and I will make you into
> a nation greater and mightier than they.
> (Numbers 14:12)

Chrysostomos was quite fond of a young playwright, Georgios Kotzioulas, the director of a troupe of travelling players who were also resistance fighters. While the bishop was inspiring Christians to save Jews with words of love and compassion, the resistance was inspiring people to action with dreams of revolution and visions of a social utopia. Historian Mark Mazower summarized one of Kotzioulas' plays, *Ta Pathi ton Evraion* (The Sufferings of the Jews):

> Haim, the son of a rich merchant, and Moises, his former employee, meet on equal terms in the hills. Moises, who has joined the *andartes*, tells Haim to rid himself of his "prewar mentality." In the mountains there is no room for selfishness, or thoughts of individual profit: "Here everything is shared. We live like brothers." Haim is worried at the thought of living alongside Christians; but Moises reminds him: "Now we must change our way of life, change our habits." The Jews need not think any longer about emigrating to Palestine; the *andartes* will build a new society in Greece.[240]

Chrysostomos was skeptical of a "new society" in Greece, as the left-leaning *andartes* were facing a right-wing backlash that would lead to the Greek Civil War. The anti-communist hysteria with its nationalistic fervor and phobias would change Greek cultural and intellectual life. The country was becoming dominated by conservative politicians and the armed forces, while behind them in the shadows lurked right-wing paramilitary organizations. Later, during the military dictatorship (1967-1974), a law was passed declaring the *andartes* enemies of Greece, while making former members of the collaborationist Security Battalions eligible for state pensions. The dictatorship was run by a group of military colonels, several of whom served in the Security Battalions.

The resistance fighters were risking their lives to save Greek Jews on Zakynthos and throughout Greece, but the tragic paradox is that by the end of 1945, "ten times more *andartes* had been convicted by the courts than collaborators, and the figures steepened as the civil war escalated."[241] The idyllic utopia imagined by playwright Kotzioulas was just that – imaginary, and Chrysostomos knew it. The bishop was working furiously to save Jews. The following year, he would be working to save resistance fighters.

The impending civil war notwithstanding, the bishop and the mayor continued to marshal all their human and material resources to hasten the evacuation of Jewish families. The move was especially hard on older folks, the *yiayias* and *pappous*, many of whom were frail or sick.

The wait for Hitler's response seemed interminable. Days passed without a word from Commander Litt. And with each passing day, optimism waned. Chrysostomos had run out of options.

Dionysios Stravolemos wrote in his diary that the Germans had not abated their "violent storm of terror" on the island and that all signs "did not offer optimistic prospects." From the depths of despair, the diary revealed, "[t]he course of things changed…A great miracle happened." In jubilant, somewhat overwrought prose, Stravolemos documented the miracle:

> The announcement which they were waiting for with agony arrived. The red-fingered dawn of salvation rose. The violent storm abated. The clouds of desperation dissolved and the horizon took on the appearance of joy. The answer which came from the High Command of the Axis to the bishop's appeal explained this divine joy. The Military Administrator

called him and announced to him: "The Jews of Zakynthos will remain under the personal responsibility of the bishop and the mayor." [242]

Stravolemos captured the powerful emotions of the moment as the news quickly spread across the island:

Christians and Jews embraced, gave thanks to God and gratitude to the bishop and the mayor. These moments were worthy as were the thanks and the gratitude. These are the moments, the fragile moments, that show that one is human, to express oneself as a human being, and this community of Zakynthos showed it and expressed it. The heritage which it bequeathed to future generations of Zakynthians was sacred, lofty and great.[243]

"The Jews of Zakynthos will remain under the personal responsibility of the bishop and the mayor" were the words the bishop wanted to hear, but he remained skeptical and paranoid. Could this be a ruse, a treacherous tactic to get the Jews out of hiding? The Germans used this kind of deception in Salonika, Jannina and other places to encourage complacency and cooperation, which led to deportation and death.

The bishop and the mayor considered the news as a temporary reprieve and remained steadfast in their mission. There would be no change in strategy. The Greek Jews of Zakynthos would remain hidden until the war's end.

The bishop asked Litt for a copy of Hitler's order, which was given to him. That copy, along with many other documents of the occupation, were given to the bishop's brother-in-law after the liberation. They were stored safely in his archives, but destroyed in the fires from the earthquake in August, 1953.

With only 275 Jews on the island, some felt that the Germans wouldn't bother deporting such a small number, and that the bishop and the mayor were overreacting. But intelligence from the resistance revealed that the Germans had gone to the trouble of sending a boat to the small Aegean island of Kos to deport only 100 Jews. They also went to the distant island of Mitilini which was ten miles off the coast of Turkey to deport a handful of

Jews, while on the mainland they went to obscure places like Katerini and Soufli to deport small numbers of Jews. There is little doubt, therefore, that the saving of the Jews of Zakynthos was the result of human intervention. As historian Yitzchak Kerem points out, the German deportation policies and actions in these and other locations "...strengthens the case that the Jews of Zakynthos were saved intentionally and not accidentally."[244]

If there is a contrarian attitude about the historical truth of the saving of the Jews of Zakynthos, Kerem presents this argument:

> The element of the Führer's role and Berlin's instructions in this matter weigh as much as Litt's role and the logistics of the boats in determining why the deportation never took place. When viewing the total picture of the destruction of Greek Jewry in the Holocaust and the great extent to which Jews were deported and caught in hiding in Greece, explaining the non-existence of a deportation as an oversight appears to be a rather weak contention.[245]

Chrysostomos wasn't concerned with the reasons why the deportations were not happening. His only concern was the saving of lives. He assumed that Litt was relieved to get Hitler's order. There would be no need to scour the island for hidden Jews, no need to fight the *andartes,* no need to plan the logistics of deportation. This would be the "new normal" for the duration of the war on Zakynthos. The bishop and the mayor assumed the Allies would liberate Greece, and all the citizens of the island would survive, both Christians and Jews. In the meantime, they communicated with Litt when necessary and felt no imminent threat of danger, until August, 1944.

A German boat arrived at the port and a group of officers were spotted disembarking. Within hours, word spread that a new commander had replaced Litt. Upon discovering that Litt had compiled no records of the island's Jews, the new commander ordered three boats to deport the Jews. Word was immediately sent to the *andartes* to prepare for confrontations.

The next day, the bishop and the mayor were called to appear before the new German officials. The bishop explained that there were no Jews in the city as they had already fled into the mountains. The Germans threatened to kill the mayor and demanded a list of all the Jews. That very night, mayor Carrer fled the island by boat under cover of night. He went to another island and did not return until after the liberation.

The bishop saw no sign of Litt. He learned later that the man had been arrested and put in prison. It is unknown what exactly happened to Litt after his arrest, but some accounts claim he was killed several days before the end of the German occupation while others say he was put on trial in Salonika by the Germans for not deporting the Jews of Zakynthos.[246]

A month after Litt's ignominious and mysterious departure, Chrysostomos was given a message from the British to be delivered to the Germans. It was a demand for the Germans to surrender. The message also called for the resistance group EAM/ELAS to surrender all of its arms.

From September 4 through 10, 1944 chaos reigned on the island. The retreating Germans were attacking people indiscriminately, looting and vandalizing as they left. They burned homes and buildings, including a church. They planted land mines, hoping to kill as many as possible. Guerilla snipers shot at them as they left, while British planes attacked from the air. On September 12, Zakynthos was officially liberated by the British.

Judaic studies professor Stephen Bowman emphasized in his writings that Greece has the distinction of being the first liberated state of any European country to provide fair and just resolution of the problem of Nazi confiscated Jewish property. "In 1946," he wrote, "the Greek government passed a law restoring to the Jewish community the heirless properties of those Jews who had been deported to the death camps of Poland...a problem about which Jewish organizations in Britain, the United States and Palestine were quite concerned during the war."[247]

The saving of the Jews of Zakynthos has been called a miracle. But it was neither an act of God nor a phenomenon of nature, but rather a remarkable demonstration of human courage and compassion -- a modern parable of good people doing good deeds that saved lives. Bishop Chrysostomos and Mayor Carrer were two of those good people, but there were many others, both

Christian and Jew. And then there were those who did nothing, but to their credit, said nothing. Of the 42,000 residents of Zakynthos, not a single person said a single word about who was Jewish or where Jews were hiding. No one said a word during the entire three-and-a-half-year occupation. That in itself could be considered a miracle.

Bishop Chrysostomos died in October, 1957. Twenty-one years later, his sister, Vasiliki Stravolemos, received a letter from Moshe Beoski, President of the Committee of the Righteous Among the Nations at Yad Vashem, which read in part:

> I have the honor to inform you that the "Committee of the Righteous"...has decided, after previous research, to award to your deceased brother, Chrisostomos [sic] (Archbishop of Zakynthos) the medal of "Righteous," for the bravery and the humane aid which he displayed, saving Jews, with danger to his life, while under the German occupation.[248]

Mayor Carrer received a similar letter and on November 7, 1978, the Israeli Ambassador to

Greece, Nissin Giais, presented the awards at the Embassy of Israel in Athens. His presentation included these eloquent remarks:

> By their example, they gave the world living proof, within the darkest moments of existence, that moral values, and the belief in the sanctity of human life, had not been eradicated. As long as there are people like Archbishop Chrisostomos [sic] and Loukas Carrer...there exists hope that the powers of humaneness and civilization will triumph over the powers of darkness and barbarism.[249]

The earthquakes and fires of 1953 destroyed the entire island, including all documents and photographs of the occupation years. A cruel act of nature and the dense fog of time have obscured history. Memory, individual and institutional, has faded. Post-war generations have scant knowledge of what happened on their island seventy years ago. Young librarians at the Zakynthos library never heard of Bishop Chrysostomos or Mayor Loukas Carrer. Few tourists visit the statues of the bishop and the mayor on Tertseti Street, at the site of the former synagogue. For years, textbooks in schools throughout Greece omitted mention of the Holocaust. Remembrance became the province of scholars, historians, diplomats, inquisitive students, survivors and their families.

Fortunately, Holocaust education is being revived in Greece. For example, in June, 2014, the Jewish Museum of Greece organized the twelfth Seminar on Holocaust Education. It was designed for primary and secondary school teachers and was conducted under the auspices of the Greek Ministry of Education and Religion. The two-day seminar, open to the public, was held in Zakynthos. Participants were eager to learn about the Holocaust in Greece, about the saving of the Jews on their own island and about the men and women honored as "Righteous Among the Nations" -- 321 Greeks, more than was awarded to citizens of Austria, Bulgaria, Croatia, Macedonia and Romania combined.

In Salonika, where over ninety percent of the city's 54,000 Jews perished, the University of Thessaloniki established educational programs to explore the community's history and culture.

On the 27th of January each year, the Greek Parliament commemorates the National Day of Remembrance for Victims and Heroes of the Holocaust. On January 22, 2014, the Greek Ministry of Education and Religion issued a memorandum stating its aim "to contribute to the preservation of the memory of the Holocaust and to combat anti-Semitism and racism, to support the training of educators in teaching about the Holocaust in Greek schools, and to organize activities which promote greater sensitivity of the citizens in these issues."[250] In 2013, senior high school students from Athens and Salonika made the first educational visit to the Auschwitz Memorial Museum. After the visit, a student wrote this impression:

> After the visit I realized that indifference never solves anything; it was the indifference of many that cost so many lives. Now I know that we can and should fight to save ourselves, or failing that, those who come after us. Even when times are hard, we should never give up or shut our eyes or turn our backs on our neighbors.[251]

The story of Zakynthos is about moral issues and human behavior. It illustrates what it means to be a responsible citizen, to show empathy and to take action. It teaches that there can be no faith, creed, code of ethics, legal or political system that endorses silence and indifference to the pain and suffering of other human beings. The grandson of Mayor Carrer, Alexandros Kriezis-Carrer, wrote that the actions of his grandfather and Bishop Chrysostomos "…carry a message of compassion for all human beings. It is not Jews that my grandfather helped to save. It was people. Humans. Men, women and children…it is a story of two men, with an all encompassing compassion in their hearts, who were ready to sacrifice their lives in order to save their fellow human beings, irrespective of their religious beliefs."[252]

The Holocaust was not an accident. It happened because individuals, governments, churches and organizations made choices that summoned the darkest of angels to corrupt human thought and behavior, resulting in discrimination, prejudice, hatred and mass murder.

Bishop Chrysostomos and Mayor Loukas Carrer made choices, took action and saved lives.

Their friends and neighbors became the only Greek Jewish community in all of Greece to survive in its entirety from annihilation. That legacy is worth remembering, and the lesson worth teaching.

ACKNOWLEDGMENTS

I thank Daphna Szanto for providing the translations from Hebrew, and Marcia Haddad Ikonomopoulos for the translations from Greek.

My heartfelt gratitude goes to the people of Zakynthos who shared their poignant remembrances with me.

A number of scholars and friends gave me information, advice and encouragement. I am especially grateful to Samuel Mordos, Pavlos and Athina Kontostavlakis, Yitzchak Kerem, Rev. Stanley Harakas, Alex Moissis, Anastasia Loudarou, Anna Bayer, Alexandros Kriezis-Carrer, Cynthia Ramsay, Judith Cohen, Jackie and Taki at Nefis Travel, Calliope Toufidou, Takis Tetradis, Harold Leich, Jeorge Seder, Dick Bangham, Veronica Vannoy, Emily Heinlen, Guillaume Bernardeau, Georghios Tembrios, Vivian Keramidas, and Tom Kaufman.

The Jewish Museum of Greece was very helpful in providing information and materials that were saved from the earthquakes and fires of 1953. Also helpful in providing survivor testimonies and research material were the archives of the U.S. Holocaust Memorial Museum, Yad Vashem, the USC Shoah Foundation, the YIVO Institute for Jewish Research, the Museum of Jewish Heritage and the Library of Congress.

Thank you Nancy and Ellis J. Parker, Kirstyn Kralovec, Dave Lilling and Cultural Exchange Foundation for your generous support.

And special thanks to my wife and editor, Anita Semjen, who forced me to write and rewrite until I got it right.

BIBLIOGRAPHY

Books

Benda, Julien, *The Treason of the Intellectuals*, (W.W. Norton, Co., New York, 1928).

Bettelheim, Bruno, "Individual and Mass Behavior in Extreme Situations," cited in Eleanor E. Maccabee, Theodore M. Newcomb,

Eugene L. Hartley, *Readings in Social Psychology*, (Hold, Reinehart and Winston, New York, 1958).

Bickerman, Elias J., *The Jews in the Greek Age*, (Harvard University Press, Cambridge, MA, 1988).

Bowman, Steven, *The Agony of Greek Jews*, (Stanford University Press, Stanford, CA, 2009).

_____, *Jewish Resistance in Wartime Greece*, (Valentine Mitchell, London, 2006).

Chadwick, Owen, *Britain and the Vatican during the Second World War*, (Cambridge University Press, Cambridge, England, 1986).

Cobb, Richard, *The People's Army*, (Yale University, New Haven, 1987).

Constantopoulou, Photini, and Veremis, Thanos, ed., *Documents on the History of the Greek Jews; Records from the Historical Archives of the Ministry of Foreign Affairs*, (Kastaniotis Editions, Athens, 2001).

Fettman, Cantor Leo, *Shoah, Journey from the Ashes*, (Six Points Press, Omaha, NE, 1999).

Fleming, K. E., *Greece: A Jewish History*, (Princeton University Press, Princeton, NJ, 2008).

Fonseca, Isabel, *Bury Me Standing, The Gypsies and Their Journey*, (Vintage Books, New York, 1995).

Giesen, Bernard, et al., *Cultural Trauma and Collective Identity*, (University of California Press, Berkeley, 2004).

_____, "The Trauma of Perpetrators, The Holocaust as the Traumatic Reference of German National Identity," published in Roy F. Baumeister, *Evil, Inside Human Violence and Cruelty*, (Henry Holt, New York, 1999).

Grunwald-Spier, Agnes, *The Other Schindlers: Why Some People Chose to Save Jews in the Holocaust*, (The History Press, Stroud, Gloucestershire, 2010).

Hancock, Ian, Ph.D., *We Are the Romani People*, (University of

Bibliography

Hertfordshire Press, Hatfield, GB, 2013).

Hausner, Gideon, *Justice in Jerusalem*, (Harper & Row, New York, 1966).

Hondros, John Louis, *Occupation and Resistance, The Greek Agony 1941-44*, (Pella Publishing Company, New York, 1983).

Lengyel, Olga, *Five Chimneys: A Woman Survivor's Story of Auschwitz*, (Academy Chicago Publishers, Chicago, 1947).

Lewy, Guenter, *The Catholic Church and Nazi Germany*, (Da Capo Press, New York, 1964).

Lipstadt, Deborah E., *The Eichman Trial*, (Schocken Books, New York, 2011).

Michael Matsas, *The Illusion of Safety: The Story of the Greek Jews During World War II*, (Pella Publishing Company, Inc., New York).

Mazower, Mark, *Inside Hitler's Greece: The Experience of Occupation, 1941-1944*, (Yale University Press, New Haven, CT, 2001).

McGuckin, John Anthony, *The Orthodox Church*, (John Wiley, Chichester, UK, 2011).

Moissis, Asher, *Greek-Jewish Patrimony*, (CreateSpace, North Charleston, SC, 2012).

Nyiszli, Dr. Miklos, *Auschwitz, A Doctor's Eyewitness Account*, (Arcade Publishing, New York, 1960).

Papademetriou, George C., *Essays on Orthodox Christian-Jewish Relations*, (Wyndam Hall Press, Bristol, England, 1990).

Philip Schaff (ed.), *Nicene and Post-Nicene Fathers of the Christian Church*, (William B. Eerdmans Co., Grand Rapids, 1956), Vol. III.

Sciolino, Anthony J., *The Holocaust, the Church, and the Law of Unintended Consequences, How Christian Anti-Judaism Spawned Nazi Anti-Semitism*, (iUniverse, Bloomington, 2012).

Silver, Eric, *The Book of the Just: The Silent Heroes Who Saved Jews from Hitler*, (Weidenfeld and Nicolson, London, 1992).

Stravolemos, Dionysios, *An Act of Heroism—A Justification; The Saving of the Jews of Zakynthos During the Occupation*, trans. Marcia Haddad Ikonomopoulos, (Athenai, Zakynthos, Greece, 1988).

Stravolemos, Dionysios, *Zakynthos During the Years of Slavery*, trans. Marcia Haddad Ikonomopoulos, (Zakynthos, Greece, 1949).

Vickers, Hugo, *Alice, Princess Andrew of Greece*, (Hamish Hamilton, London, 2000).

Victor, George, *Hitler: The Pathology of Evil*, (Potomac Books, Washington, DC, 2007).

Wiesel, Elie and Heffner, Richard D., *Conversations with Elie Wiesel*, (Shocken Books, New York, 2001).

Wills, Gary, *Papal Sin*, (Doubleday, New York, 2000).

Articles

Agourides, Savas, "The Social Character of Orthodoxy," A. J. Philippou, ed., *The Orthodox Ethos*, (Holywell Press, Oxford, England, 1964).

Altsech, Moses B., "Greek Jews and the Holocaust, " Journal of the Hellenic Diaspora, Vol. 23.2, 1997.

Andrew Apostolou, "The Betrayal of Salonika's Jews," *Jewish Ideas Daily*, April 18, 2013,
http://www.jewishideasdaily.com/6341/features/the-betrayal-of-salonikas-jews/.

Bowman, Steven, "Jews in Wartime Greece," *Jewish Social Studies*, Vol. 48, No. 1, 1986.

Cohen, Dr. Phillip J., "Serbia's Nazi Past and Genocide Against Jews in the Holocaust," *Mindstream, A Monthly Jewish Review*, Vol. XXXVIII, No. 8, Nov. 1992.

Constantelos, Demetrios J., Ph.D., "Theological Considerations for the Social Ethos of the Orthodox Church," *Journal of Ecumenical Studies*, Temple University, Vol. XI, Number 1, 33.

Eptakili, Tassoula, "The Greek island that hid its Jews from the Nazis," www.ekathimerini.com, July 11, 2014.

Harakas, Rev. Stanley S., Th.D., D.D., Dean of Holy Cross School of Theology, (ret.), "The Orthodox Christian Tradition," Park Ridge Center for the Study of Health, Faith and Ethics, Chicago, 1999.

Ikonomopoulos, Marcia Haddad, "The Story Behind the Statistics: Variables Affecting the Tremendous Losses of Greek Jewry During the Holocaust," *Journal of the Hellenic Diaspora*, New York, NY, Vol. 32. 1 & 2, 2006, 103.

The International Raoul Wallenberg Foundation, New York, "Archbishop Damaskinos and the Jewish Holocaust," (www.raoulwallenberg.net/es/ generales/archbishop-damaskinos).

The International Raoul Wallenberg Foundation, New York, "The Greek Orthodox Church and the Academic World of the Greek People Protest against the Persecution of Greek Jewry," (http://www.raoulwallenberg.net/general/greek-orthodox-church-academic).

Kay, Richard, "Revealed: Secret Heroism of Prince Philip's Mother,"
Daily Mail, July 26, 1993.

Kendal, Jonathan, "Kurt Waldheim at 88; ex-UN chief hid Nazi past,"
New York Times, June 14, 2007.

Kerem, Yitzchak, "The Role of Greek Righteous Gentiles in the Rescue
of Greek Jews in the Holocaust," *Gesher, Bridge, The Official Journal of
the Council of Christians & Jews,* Vol. I, No. 4, October, 1944.
_____ , "The Survival of the Jews of Zakynthos,"
Proceedings of the World Congress of Jewish Studies, Div. B, Vol. II, "The
History of the Jewish People," World Union of Jewish Studies, 1990.

Kitroeff, Alexandros, "Documents: The Jews in Greece, 1941-1944 –
Eyewitness Accounts," *Journal of the Hellenic Diaspora,* Vol. XII, No. 3,
Fall, 1985.

Kevin Knight, "Beatification and Canonization," *New Advent Catholic
Encyclopedia,* http://www.newadvent.org/cathen/02364b.htm.

Dariusz Libionka, "The Catholic Church in Poland and the Holocaust,
1939-1945," *The Holocaust and the Christian World,* Yad Vashem, 2000.

"Our Eyes Have Been Cloaked," *Catholic Herald,* May 14, 1965,

"Pope Pius XII Refused to Intervene for Jews Under Nazis, U.S.
Reveals," *Jewish Telegraphic Agency,* May 15, 1961.

Sheramy, Roma, "Nechama Tec," *Jewish Women: A Comprehensive
Historical Encyclopedia,"* March 1, 2009, Jewish Women's Archive,
http://jwa.org/encyclopedia/article/tec-nechama.

United States Holocaust Memorial Museum, Washington, DC, "The
Holocaust in Greece," http://www.ushmm.org/m/pdfs/20130305-
holocaust-in-greece.pdf.

Ware, Bishop Kallistos, "The Communion of Saints," A. J. Philippou,
ed., *The Orthodox Ethos,* (Holywell Press, Oxford, England, 1964).

Yad Vashem, "The Righteous Among The Nations; Rescue in the Royal
Palace, Princess Alice, Greece,"
www.yadvashem.org/yv/en/righteous/stories/princess_alice.asp.

Survivor Testimonies

Interview of Angel Mirou-Mairy, 2006, *Centropa Interviews,*
www.centropa.org/biography/angel-mirou-mairy.

Interview of Erkanas Tsezana, 1998, from the archive of the USC
Shoah Foundation, Code 39196, Los Angeles.

Interview of Ester Dante, 1995, from the archive of the United States Holocaust Memorial Museum, Code 1995.A.1272.231, Washington, D.C.

Interview of Hertsel Matsa, 1996, from the archive of the USC Shoah Foundation, Code 16634, Los Angeles.

Interview of Lily Arouch, 2005, *Centropa Interview,* www.centropa.org/biography/lily-arouch.

Interview of Malvina Messina, 1998, from the archive of the USC Shoah Foundation, Code 38981, Los Angeles.

Interview of Raphael Constantinos, 2001, from the archive of Yad Vashem, Code VT 5738, Jerusalem.

Interview of Shlomo Amar, 2005, from the archive of Yad Vashem, Code VT 10572, Jerusalem.

Interviews

Interview of Rev. Stanley S. Harakas, Th.D., D.D., Dean of Holy Cross School of Theology, (ret.), by the author, Nov. 4, 2013.

Interview of Takis Tetradis, by the author, Washington, D.C., June 13, 2014.

Documents

Deborah Renee Altamirano, "Up in Arms: The Lives and Times of Women Activists in the World War II Greek Resistance," Ph.D. thesis, University of California at Santa Barbara, March, 1993.

BBC, "1943: Italy's surrender announced," http://news.bbc.co.uk/onthisday/ hi/dates/stories/September/8/newsid_3612000/3612037.stm.

Bulletin of the Italian General Consulate, November 8, 1942, Salonika, in *Italian Diplomatic Documents,* 1942.

Kriezis-Carrer, Alexandros, letter to the author, August 8, 2014.

Nuremberg Trial Proceedings, Volume 10, Testimony of Field Marshal, Defendant Wilhelm Keitel.

Correspondence from the American Consulate-General in Istanbul, Turkey, addressed to the Secretary of State, Washington, *The Foreign Service of the United States of America,* Report No. 1083 (R-922), August 7, 1943.

Katevatis, Nicholas D., M.D., letter to the Israeli Embassy in Athens, February 6, 1978, from the archive of Yad Vashem, Ref. No. 280698.

Films and Exhibitions

Lykouresis, Tony, Director, "The Song of Life," (documentary film), 2002, Greek Film Center, Greek Ministry of Foreign Affairs, Athens.

Rotter, Sy, Director, "It Was Nothing…It Was Everything: Reflections on the Rescue of Greek Jews During the Holocaust," (documentary film), 1997, Documentaries International Film & Video Foundation and Yad Vashem.

"Synagonistis, Greek Jews in the National Resistance," An Exhibition of the Jewish Museum of Greece, April 16, 2013 to April 25, 2014, Athens, Greece.

NOTES

CHAPTER 1
WILL I SEE YOU TOMORROW?

[1] Interview of Malvina Messina, 1998, from the archive of the USC Shoah Foundation, Code 38981, Los Angeles.

[2] Interview of Erkanas Tsezana, 1998, from the archive of the USC Shoah Foundation, Code 39196, Los Angeles.

[3] The International Raoul Wallenberg Foundation, New York, "The Greek Orthodox Church and the Academic World of the Greek People Protest against the Persecution of Greek Jewry," (http://www.raoulwallenberg.net/general/greek-orthodox-church-academic).

[4] Ibid.

[5] United States Holocaust Memorial Museum, Washington, DC, "The Holocaust in Greece," http://www.ushmm.org/m/pdfs/20130305-holocaust-in-greece.pdf.

[6] Bernard Giesen, et al., *Cultural Trauma and Collective Identity*, (University of California Press, Berkeley, 2004), 114.

[7] Mark Mazower, *Inside Hitler's Greece: The Experience of Occupation, 1941-1944* (Yale University Press, New Haven, CT, 2001), 257.

[8] John Cornwell, *Hitler's Pope: The Secret History of Pius XII*, (Penguin, New York, 1999), 265.

[9] Agnes Grunwald-Spier, *The Other Schindlers: Why Some People Chose to Save Jews in the Holocaust*, (The History Press, Stroud, Gloucestershire, 2010), 17.

[10] John Donne, "Devotions Upon Emergent Occasions," 1624.

[11] Mazower, 2001, 22.

[12] *New York Times*, March 1, 1942.

Notes

[13] Stephen G. Xidis, *The Economy and Finances of Greece under Occupation* (Greek Government Office of Information, 1944), 12.

[14] Tsezana, 1998.

[15] Tsezana, 1998.

[16] Interview of Raphael Constantinos, 2001, from the archive of Yad Vashem, Code VT-5738, Jerusalem.

[17] Tsezana, 1998.

[18] Interview of Hertsel Matsa, 1996, from the archive of the USC Shoah Foundation, Code 16634, Los Angeles.

[19] Interview of Takis Tetradis by the author, Washington, D.C., June 13, 2014.

[20] Mazower, 2001, 150.

[21] John Louis Hondros, *Occupation and Resistance, The Greek Agony 1941-44*, (Pella Publishing Company, New York, 1983), 62-63.

[22] Records Group, 1016 and 1026, German Armed Forces High Command, Economic and Armament Office, (OKW/Wi Rue Amt), "Greece File": Wi/C1.40 (KTB VO OKW/Wi. Rue. Amt. AOK 12 (IV Wi), July 7 — December 31, 1941), W. B. Suedost IV Wi to OKW/Wi Rue. Amt., October 9, 1941 cited in Hondros, 1983, 63.

[23] Michael Molho and Joseph Nehama, *In Mémoriam, Hommage aux victims juives des Nazis Grèce* (Salonique: N. Nicolaides, 1948-19490, Vol. 1), 2-12, 22-28, cited in Hondros, 1983, 91.

[24] Tsezana, 1998.

[25] Steven Bowman, *Jewish Resistance in Wartime Greece*, (Valentine Mitchell, London, 2006), viii.

[26] Deborah Renee Altamirano, "Up in Arms: The Lives and Times of Women Activists in the World War II Greek Resistance," Ph.D. thesis, University of California at Santa Barbara, March, 1993.

[27] Bowman, 2006, 34.

[28] Asher Moissis, *Greek-Jewish Patrimony*, (CreateSpace, North Charleston, SC, 2012), 72-73.

[29] K. E. Fleming, *Greece: A Jewish History*, (Princeton University Press, Princeton, NJ, 2008), 183.

[30] Mazower, 2001, 297.

[31] Hondros, 1983, 84.

[32] Richard Cobb, *The People's Army*, (Yale University, New Haven, 1987), cited in Mazower, 2001, 223.

[33] Michael Matsas, *The Illusion of Safety: The Story of the Greek Jews During World War II*, (Pella Publishing Company, Inc., New York, 19), 276.

[34] Ibid., 277.

[35] Mazower, 2001, 153.

[36] Ibid., 127-128.

[37] Nicholas D. Katevatis, M.D., letter to the Israeli Embassy in Athens, February 6, 1978, from the archives of Yad Vashem, Ref. No. 280698

[38] Ibid.

[39] Ibid.

[40] Ian Hancock, Ph.D., *We Are the Romani People*, (University of Hertfordshire Press, Hatfield, GB, 2013), 30.

[41] Ibid., 35.

[42] Ibid., 42.

[43] Isabel Fonseca, *Bury Me Standing, The Gypsies and Their Journey*, (Vintage Books, New York, 1995), 243.

[44] Tsezana, 1988.

CHAPTER 2
ETHOS

[45] Savas Agourides, "The Social Character of Orthodoxy," A. J. Philippou, ed., *The Orthodox Ethos*, (Holywell Press, Oxford, England, 1964), 214.

[46] Interview of Rev. Stanley S. Harakas, Th.D., D.D., Dean of Holy Cross School of Theology, (ret.), by the author, Nov. 4, 2013.

[47] Ibid.

[48] Demetrios J. Constantelos, Ph.D., "Theological Considerations for the Social Ethos of the Orthodox Church," Journal of Ecumenical Studies, Temple University, Vol. XI, Number 1, 33.

[49] Bishop Kallistos Ware, "The Communion of Saints," A. J. Philippou, ed., *The Orthodox Ethos*, (Holywell Press, Oxford, England, 1964), 141.

[50] Anthony J. Sciolino, *The Holocaust, the Church, and the Law of Unintended Consequences, How Christian Anti-Judaism Spawned Nazi Anti-Semitism*, (iUniverse, Bloomington, 2012), 2.

[51] Philip Schaff (ed.), *Nicene and Post-Nicene Fathers of the Christian Church*, (William B. Eerdmans Co., Grand Rapids, 1956), Vol III, 373.

[52] Sciolino, 2012, 13.

[53] *Luther's Works*, Vol. 47, *The Christian in Society IV*, cited in Cantor Leo Fettman, *Shoah, Journey from the Ashes*, (Six Points Press, Omaha, NE, 1999), xiv.

[54] George C. Papademetriou, *Essays on Orthodox Christian-Jewish Relations*, (Wyndam Hall Press, Bristol, England, 1990), 88.

[55] Cantor Leo Fettman, *Shoah, Journey from the Ashes*, (Six Points Press, Omaha, NE, 1999), xvi.

[56] Ibid., xvii.

[57] Ibid., xi.

[58] Sciolino, 2012, 174.

[59] Deborah E. Lipstadt, *The Eichman Trial*, (Schocken Books, New York, 2011), 185.

[60] Interview of Shlomo Amar, 2005, from the archive of Yad Vashem, Code VT 10572, Jerusalem.

[61] Interview of Malvina Messina, 1998, from the archive of the USC Shoah Foundation, Code 38981, Los Angeles.

[62] Matsa, 1996.

[63] Rev. Stanley S. Harakas, Th.D., D.D., Dean of Holy Cross School of Theology, (ret.), "The Orthodox Christian Tradition," Park Ridge Center for the Study of Health, Faith and Ethics, Chicago, 1999, 3.

[64] Fleming, 2008, 92.

[65] Photini Constantopoulou, Thanos Veremis, ed., *Documents on the History of the Greek Jews; Records from the Historical Archives of the Ministry of Foreign Affairs,* (Kastaniotis Editions, Athens, 2001), 175.

[66] Fleming, 2008, 98.

[67] *Ausw. Amt. Staatssekretaer Grld.,* Altenburg to Ribbentrop, May 8, 1941; T-120, Roll 257, Frames 127545-127546, cited in Hondros, 1983, 79.

[68] Hondros, 1983, 79.

[69] Andrew Apostolou, "The Betrayal of Salonika's Jews," *Jewish Ideas Daily*, April 18, 2013, http://www.jewishideasdaily.com/6341/features/the-betrayal-of-salonikas-jews/

[70] John Anthony McGuckin, *The Orthodox Church,* (John Wiley & Sons, Chichester, UK, 2011), 402.

[71] Constantinopoulou and Veremis, 2001, 276.

[72] Dr. Philip J. Cohen, "Serbia's Nazi Past and Genocide Against Jews in the Holocaust," *Mindstream, A Monthly Jewish Review,* Vol. XXXVIII, No. 8, Nov. 1992.

[73] Dariusz Libionka, "The Catholic Church in Poland and the Holocaust, 1939-1945," *Reflections on the Past, Challenges for the Future,* Yad Vashem, Jerusalem, 2000, 74.

[74] "Pope Pius XII Refused to Intervene for Jews Under Nazis, U.S. Reveals," *Jewish Telegraphic Agency*, May 15, 1961.

[75] Owen Chadwick, *Britain and the Vatican during the Second World War,* (Cambridge University Press, Cambridge, England, 1986), 217.

[76] Guenter Lewy, *The Catholic Church and Nazi Germany*, (Da Capo Press, New York, 1964), 303.

[77] Chadwick, 1986, 216.

[78] Ibid., 216.

[79] Ibid., xix.

[80] Cornwell, 2008, 316.

[81] Sciolino, 2012, 163.

[82] "Our Eyes Have Been Cloaked," *Catholic Herald*, May 14, 1965, 1.

[83] Kevin Knight, "Beatification and Canonization," *New Advent Catholic Encyclopedia*, http://www.newadvent.org/cathen/02364b.htm.

[84] Gary Wills, *Papal Sin*, (Doubleday, New York, 2000), 13.

[85] Quoted in S. Shapiro, "Hearing the Testimony of Radical Negation," *The Holocaust as Interruption* (Edinburgh, 1984), 3-4.

[86] Grunwald-Spier, 2010, 102.

CHAPTER 3
PATHOS

[87] Eric Silver, *The Book of the Just: The Silent Heroes Who Saved Jews from Hitler*, (Weidenfeld and Nicolson, London, 1992), 147.

[88] Roma Sheramy, "Nechama Tec," *Jewish Women: A Comprehensive Historical Encyclopedia,"* March 1, 2009, Jewish Women's Archive, http://jwa.org/encyclopedia/article/tec-nechama.

[89] Elie Wiesel and Richard D. Heffner, *Conversations with Elie Wiesel*, (Shocken Books, New York, 2001), 14.

[90] Edmund Burke, *Thoughts on the Cause of the Present Discontents*, 1770, 71.

[91] George Victor, *Hitler: The Pathology of Evil*, (Potomac Books, Washington, DC, 2007, 85.

[92] Bernard Giesen, "The Trauma of Perpetrators, The Holocaust as the Traumatic Reference of German National Identity," published in Roy F. Baumeister, *Evil, Inside Human Violence and Cruelty*, Henry Holt, New York, 1999), 114.

[93] Julien Benda, *The Treason of the Intellectuals*, (W.W. Norton, Co., NY, 1928), 5.

[94] Ibid., 27.

[95] Nuremberg Trial Proceedings, Volume 10, Testimony of Field Marshal, Defendant Wilhelm Keitel.

[96] Lipstadt, 2011, 183.

[97] Moissis, 2012, 15.

[98] Ibid., 27.

[99] Ibid., 12.

[100] Ibid., 170.

[101] Victor, 2007, 20.

CHAPTER 4
OCCUPATION

[102] Hondros, 1983, 154.

[103] Ibid., 155, 158.

[104] Dionysios Stravolemos, *Zakynthos During the Years of Slavery*, (trans. Marcia Haddad Ikonomopoulos, Zakynthos, Greece, 1949), 46.

[105] Ibid., 51.

[106] Ibid., 105.

[107] BBC, "1943: Italy's surrender announced," http://news.bbc.co.uk/onthisday/ hi/dates/stories/September/8/newsid_3612000/3612037.stm

[108] Hondros, 1983, 82-83.

[109] Interview of Raphael Constantinos, 2001, from the archive of Yad Vashem, Code VT 5738, Jerusalem.

[110] Amar, 2005.

[111] Alexandros Kitroeff, "Documents: The Jews in Greece, 1941-1944 – Eyewitness Accounts," (*Journal of the Hellenic Diaspora*, Vol. XII, No. 3, Fall, 1985), 29.

[112] Amar, 2005.

[113] Constantinopoulou and Veremis, 2001, 277.

[114] Ibid., 277.

[115] Ibid., 278.

[116] G. Christodoulou, Consul in charge for Palestine and Trans-Jordan, to the Ministry of Foreign Affairs, Confidential Letter, Jerusalem, June 1, 1944, cited in Constantinopoulou and Veremis, 2001, 291.

[117] Marcia Haddad Ikonomopoulos, "The Story Behind the Statistics: Variables Affecting the Tremendous Losses of Greek Jewry During the Holocaust," *Journal of the Hellenic Diaspora*, New York, NY, Vol. 32. 1 & 2, 2006, 103.

[118] Olga Lengyel, *Five Chimneys: A Woman Survivor's Story of Auschwitz*, (Academy Chicago Publishers, Chicago, 1947).

[119] Steven Bowman, "Jews in Wartime Greece," *Jewish Social Studies*, Vol. 48, No. 1, 1986.

[120] Ibid., 53.

[121] Moses B. Altsech, "Greek Jews and the Holocaust, " Journal of the Hellenic Diaspora, Vol. 23.2, 1997, 53-54.

[122] Ibid., 56-57.

[123] Ibid., 59.

[124] Ibid., 60.

[125] Fleming, 2008, 119.

[126] Bulletin of the Italian General Consulate, November 8, 1942, Salonika, in *Italian Diplomatic Documents*, 1942, 24, 116.

[127] Matsas, 1997, 45.

[128] Interview of Angel Mirou-Mairy, 2006, *Centropa Interviews,*
www.centropa.org/biography/angel-mirou-mairy. 15.

[129] Interview of Lily Arouch, 2005, *Centropa Interviews,*
www.centropa.org/biography/lily-arouch, 9.

[130] Ibid., 49.

[131] Ibid., 58.

[132] Moissis, 2012, 16.

[133] Molho and Nehama, 1983, cited in Constantopoulou and Veremis,
2001, 35.

[134] Moissis, 2012, 87.

[135] Marcos Nahon, "Birkenau, the Death Camp," (Thessaloniki, 1991),
36.

[136] Correspondence from the American Consulate-General in Istanbul,
Turkey, addressed to the Secretary of State, Washington, *The Foreign
Service of the United States of America,* Report No. 1083 (R-922), August
7, 1943, cited in Alexandros Kitroeff, "Documents: The Jews in Greece,
1941-1944 – Eyewitness Accounts," (Journal of the Hellenic Diaspora,
Vol. XII, No. 3, Fall, 1985), 17-18.

[137] Dr. Albert Menasse, "The Story of Inmate No. 124454, *Birkenau,*
(The Greek Jewish Community of Salonika, Typo Elilinismou,
Salonika, 1974), cited in Matsas, 231-232.

[138] Dr. Miklos Nyiszli, *Auschwitz, A Doctor's Eyewitness Account,*
(Arcade Publishing, New York, 1960), 83.

[139] Altsech, 1997, 44-45.

[140] Mazower, 2001, 244.

[141] Fleming, 2008, 125.

[142] "Synagonistis, Greek Jews in the National Resistance," An
Exhibition of the Jewish Museum of Greece, April 16, 2013 to April 25,
2014 in the Jewish Museum of Greece, Athens, Greece, 14.

¹⁴³ Ibid., citing Archives of the Communist Party of Greece (KKE), Proclamation of the National Solidarity in Athens, March, 1943.

¹⁴⁴ Fleming, 2008, 140.

¹⁴⁵ Bracha Rivlin, *Encyclopedia of Jewish Communities: Greece*, (Jerusalem, 1998), 140, cited in Fleming, 2008, 140.

¹⁴⁶ Molho and Nehama, 1983, 136, cited in Fleming, 2008, 140.

¹⁴⁷ Hondros, 1983, 81 citing Wi/1.C1.4, Rallis Government, August 3, 1943, OKW/Wi Rue Amt records for Greece.

¹⁴⁸ Fleming, 2008, 136.

¹⁴⁹ Hondros, 1983, 82.

¹⁵⁰ Ikonomopoulos, 2006, 96.

¹⁵¹ Ikonomopoulos, 2006, 96.

¹⁵² Bruno Bettelheim, "Individual and Mass Behavior in Extreme Situations," cited in Eleanor E. Maccabee, Theodore M. Newcomb, Eugene L. Hartley, *Readings in Social Psychology*, (Hold, Reinehart and Winston, New York, 1958), 301.

¹⁵³ Ibid., 304.

¹⁵⁴ Dionysios, *An Act of Heroism — A Justification; The Saving of the Jews of Zakynthos During the Occupation*, (trans. Marcia Haddad Ikonomopoulos, Athenai, Zakynthos, Greece, 1988), 7.

¹⁵⁵ Moissis, 2012, 94.

CHAPTER 5
ATROCITIES

¹⁵⁶ Ibid., 9.

¹⁵⁷ Mazower, 2001, 82.

¹⁵⁸ Moissis, 2012, 10.

¹⁵⁹ Ibid., 41.

[160] Ibid., 42.

[161] Ibid., 42.

[162] Mazower, 2001, 226 citing F. Skouras *et al.*, *Psychopathologia tis peinas, tou fovou kai tou anchous: nevroseis kai psychonevroseis* (Athens, 1947), 136.

[163] Ibid., 227.

[164] Mazower, 2001, 194 citing Zentralstelle der Landesjustizverwaltungen, AR 1462/68, 105.

[165] Ibid., 163.

[166] Ibid., 86-87.

[167] Mazower, 2001, 197 citing Bundesarchiv-Militärarchiv, RH 31 X/1, Deutscher Generalstab beim ital.. A.O.K. ii, entry for 17 Aug., 1943.

[168] Ibid., 76-77.

[169] Jonathan Kendal, "Kurt Waldheim at 88; ex-UN chief hid Nazi past," *New York Times*, June 14, 2007.

[170] Mazower, 2001, 191.

[171] Ibid., 337.

[172] Ibid., 259.

[173] Hondros, 1983, 150 citing LXVIII, *Army Corps* 54961/1 (*Anlagenband z.KTB,1a,* January 1—June 30, 1944) *Ic Lagebericht*, July 11, 1944.

[174] Ibid., citing Military Commander Greece, 40131/3b, *Ic Lagebericht*, December 11, 1942; T-501 Roll 252, Frame 001042.

CHAPTER 6
THE ORDER

[175] Tony Lykouresis, "The Song of Life," (documentary film), 2002.

[176] Stravolemos, 1988, 12.

[177] Moissis, 2012, 86.

[178] The International Raoul Wallenberg Foundation, New York, "Archbishop Damaskinos and the Jewish Holocaust," (www.raoulwallenberg.net/es/ generales/archbishop-damaskinos).

[179] Yitzchak Kerem, "The Role of Greek Righteous Gentiles in the Rescue of Greek Jews in the Holocaust," *Gesher, Bridge, The Official Journal of the Council of Christians & Jews*, Vol. I, No. 4, October, 1944, 62-63.

[180] Constantinopoulou and Veremis, 2001, 296—298.

[181] Hugo Vickers, *Alice, Princess Andrew of Greece*, (Hamish Hamilton, London, 2000), 293-295.

[182] Ibid., 293.

[183] Tsouderos to Roosevelt, *Foreign Relations of the United States*, (U.S. Department of State, Vol. 2, 1941), cited in Hugo Vickers, 292.

[184] Mary Henderson, *Xenia—A Memoir*, (Weidenfeld & Nicholson, London, 1988), 47-48, cited in Hugo Vickers, 293.

[185] Vickers, 293-295.

[186] Yad Vashem, "The Righteous Among The Nations; Rescue in the Royal Palace, Princess Alice, Greece," www.yadvashem.org/yv/en/righteous/stories/princess_alice.asp.

[187] Richard Kay, "Revealed: Secret Heroism of Prince Philip's Mother," *Daily Mail*, July 26, 1993.

[188] Yad Vashem, "The Righteous Among The Nations; Rescue in the Royal Palace, Princess Alice, Greece," www.yadvashem.org/yv/en/righteous/stories/princess_alice.asp.

[189] Stravolemos, 1988, 14.

[190] Frederich Nietzsche, *The Antichrist*, § 11.

[191] Sciolino, 2012, 63.

CHAPTER 7
MALVINA MESSINA

[192] Messina, 1998.

[193] Ibid.

CHAPTER 8
RAPHAEL CONSTANTINOS

[194] Constantinos, 2001.

[195] Ibid.

[196] Ibid.

CHAPTER 9
ERKANAS TSEZANA

[197] Tsezana, 1988.

[198] Ibid.

[199] Ibid.

[200] Ibid.

[201] Ibid.

[202] Ibid.

[203] Steven Bowman, *The Agony of Greek Jews,* (Stanford University Press, Stanford, CA, 2009), 94.

[204] Ibid.

CHAPTER 10
ESTER DANTE

[205] Interview of Ester Dante, 1995, from the archive of the United States Holocaust Memorial Museum, Code 1995.A.1272.231, Washington, D.C.

[206] Ibid.

[207] Ibid.

[208] Gideon Hausner, *Justice in Jerusalem*, (Harper & Row, New York, 1966), 128, cited in Matsas, 1997, 117.

[209] Matsas, 1997, 292.

[210] Tassoula Eptakili, "The Greek island that hid its Jews from the Nazis," (www.ekathimerini.com, July 11, 2014), 2.

[211] Dante, 1995.

[212] Ibid.

[213] Ibid.

[214] Ibid.

[215] Ibid.

CHAPTER 11
THE BISHOP'S LIST

[216] United States Holocaust Memorial Museum, Washington, DC, "The Holocaust in Greece," (http://www.ushmm.org/m/pdfs/20130305-holocaust-in-greece.pdf), 18.

[217] Stravolemos, 1988, 14.

[218] Ibid., 17.

[219] Lykouresis, 2002.

[220] Ibid.

[221] Ibid.

[222] Ibid.

[223] Eptakili, 2014, 2.

[224] Stravolemos, 1988, 15.

[225] Ibid., 16.

[226] Ibid., 16.

CHAPTER 12
THE BISHOP'S LETTER

[227] Dante, 1995.

[228] Elias J. Bickerman, *The Jews in the Greek Age*, (Harvard University Press, Cambridge, MA, 1988), 25.

[229] Stravolemos, 1988, 16.

[230] Ibid., 16.

[231] Dante, 1995.

[232] Messina, 1998.

[233] Tsezana, 1998.

[234] Constantinos, 2001.

[235] Matsa, 1996.

[236] Mazower, 2001, 172.

[237] Ibid., 182-183.

[238] Ibid., 184.

[239] Mazower, 2001, 203.

[240] Ibid., 277-278 citing G. Kotzioulas, *Theatro sta vouna*, (Athens, 1976), 359, 308-9, 252-3.

[241] Ibid., 176.

[242] Stravolemos, 1988, 18.

[243] Ibid., 18.

[244] Yitzchak Kerem, "The Survival of the Jews of Zakynthos," *Proceedings of the World Congress of Jewish Studies, Div. B, Vol. II*, "This History of the Jewish People," pub. World Union of Jewish Studies, 391-392.

[245] Ibid., 393.

[246] Ibid., 392.

[247] Bowman, 2009.

[248] Stravolemos, 1988, 27.

[249] Ibid., 30.

[250] "Teaching About the Holocaust in Greece," in Zakynthos, Jewish Museum of Greece, http://www.jewishmuseum.gr/en/activities_dynamic/news/item/98.html.

[251] Ibid., http://www.jewishmuseum.gr/en/activities_dynamic/news/item/87.html

[252] Alexandros Kriezis-Carrer, letter to the author, August 8, 2014.

Made in the USA
Middletown, DE
30 October 2018